Single-Level
HOME PLANS

GARLINGHOUSE

Library of Congress: 90-85505

ISBN: 0-938708-34-1

Canadian orders should be submitted to:
The Garlinghouse Company
20 Cedar Street North
Kitchener, Ontario N2H 2W8
(519) 743-4169

TABLE OF CONTENTS

Zehr Photography

Attractive Floor Plan Enhances Traditional Design

No. 20056

This three-bedroom, two-bath home offers comfort and style. The master bedroom is complete with its own bath with a skylight. A beamed ceiling and fireplace in the living area add charm to the more traditional family room. A spacious laundry room adjoins the kitchen and breakfast area. The country-style front porch and large front windows in the breakfast and dining rooms lend a cozy atmosphere to this eye-catcher.

First floor—1,669 sq. ft.
Basement—1,669 sq. ft.
Garage—482 sq. ft.

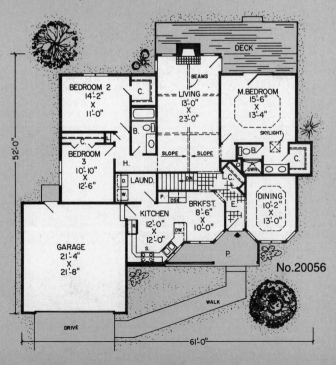

No. 20056

Circular Kitchen Is Center of Family Activities

No. 10514

The unusual design of this kitchen provides the centerpiece for this thoroughly delightful floor plan. The kitchen is further enhanced by the tiled hallways which surround it and delineate the adjacent living areas. The dining room, which opens onto the patio with large glass doors, includes both a built-in hutch and a display case. The large family room has a fireplace with its own wood storage and provides direct access to the sunspace. The master bedroom suite has a private patio, a bay window, five-piece bath, separate vanity and a large, walk-in closet. The circular kitchen floor plan has been modified by the homeowner.

Garage — 448 sq. ft.
Sunroom — 144 sq. ft.

Total living area — 1,954 sq. ft.

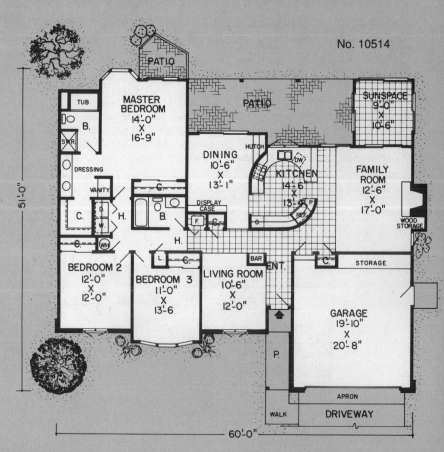

No. 10514

Westerfield Studios

Westerfield Studios

Westerfield Studios

Westerfield Studios

3

Brick-layered Home Plans 4 Bedrooms

No. 22004

Four roomy bedrooms, featuring a master bedroom with extra large bath, equip this plan for a large family or overnight guests. The centrally located family room merits a fireplace, wetbar, and access to the patio, and a dining room is provided for formal entertaining. An interesting kitchen and nook, as well as two and one half baths, are featured. Small revisions have been made by the homeowners to personalize their home.

Garage — 474 sq. ft.

Total living area — 2,070 sq. ft.

No. 22004

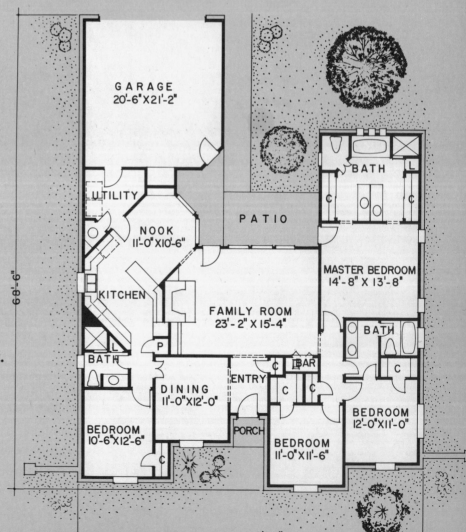

GARAGE
20'-6" X 21'-2"

UTILITY

NOOK
11'-0" X 10'-6"

PATIO

BATH

MASTER BEDROOM
14'-8" X 13'-8"

KITCHEN

FAMILY ROOM
23'-2" X 15'-4"

BATH

BATH

DINING
11'-0" X 12'-0"

ENTRY

BAR

BEDROOM
10'-6" X 12'-6"

PORCH

BEDROOM
11'-0" X 11'-6"

BEDROOM
12'-0" X 11'-0"

68'-6"

52'-0"

FLOOR PLAN

John Ehrenclou Photography

Tasteful Elegance Aim of Design

No. 22020

With an exterior that expresses French Provincial charm, this single-level design emphasizes elegance and offers a semi-circular dining area overlooking the patio. To pamper parents, the master bedroom annexes a long dressing area and private bath, while another bath serves the second and third bedrooms. A wood-burning fireplace furnishes the family room. This homeowner chose the option to build their home in reverse to best fit their site.

Garage — 469 sq. ft.

Total living area — 1,772 sq. ft.

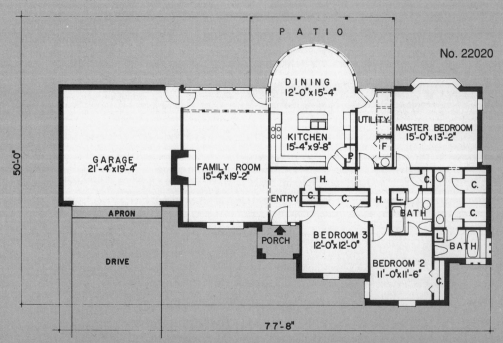

John Ehrenclou Photography

FLOOR PLAN

No. 22020

PATIO

DINING
12'-0"x15'-4"

UTILITY

MASTER BEDROOM
15'-0"x13'-2"

GARAGE
21'-4"x19'-4"

KITCHEN
15'-4"x9'-8"

F

FAMILY ROOM
15'-4"x19'-2"

P

C.

C.

H.

ENTRY

C.

H.

L.

BATH

C.

APRON

PORCH

BEDROOM 3
12'-0"x12'-0"

L.

BATH

DRIVE

BEDROOM 2
11'-0"x11'-6"

C.

50'-0"

77'-8"

Home built by Wayman Skelton

Brooks Photography

A Karl Kreeger Design

Cathedral Window Graced by Massive Arch

No. 20066

A tiled threshold provides a distinctive entrance into this spacious home. There's room for gracious living everywhere, from the comfortable living room with a wood-burning fireplace and tiled hearth, to the elegant dining room with a vaulted ceiling, to the outside deck. Plan your meals in a kitchen that has all the right ingredients: a central work island, pantry, planning desk, and breakfast area. A decorative ceiling will delight your eye in the master suite, which includes a full bath and bow window.

Basement — 1,850 sq. ft.
Garage — 503 sq. ft.

Total living area — 1,850 sq. ft.

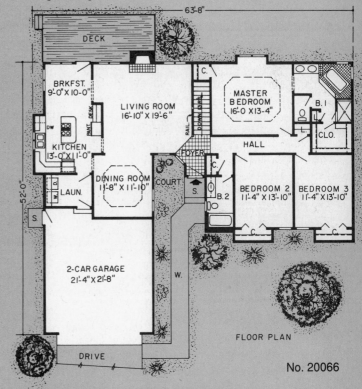

FLOOR PLAN

No. 20066

Brooks Photography

John Ehrenclou Photography

A Home for Today and Tomorrow

No. 20109

This convenient, one-level plan is perfect for the modern family with a taste for classic design. Traditional Victorian touches in this three-bedroom beauty include a romantic, railed porch and the intriguing breakfast tower just off the kitchen. But, the step-saving arrangement of the kitchen between the breakfast and formal dining rooms, the wide-open living room with sliders to a rear deck, and the handsome master suite with its skylit, compartmentalized bath make this a home you'll love today and long into the future. Notice the convenient laundry location on the bedroom hall.

Basement — 1,588 sq. ft.
Garage — 484 sq. ft.

John Ehrenclou Photography

Total living area — 1,588 sq. ft.

A Karl Kreeger Design

No. 20109

DECK

LIVING ROOM
15'-8" x 17'-0"

FAN

DINING
11'-0" x 11'-8"
SLOPE

M. BEDRM.
7-1/2" CLG. REVEAL
FAN
14'-0" x 15'-4"

PLANT SHELF
SLOPE
SHELF
B.
W D
L.
DN
L.

11'-0" CLG. HEIGHT

STOOP
UP

KITCHEN
13'-0" x 9'-0"
D.W.

FOY.
SLOPE

DEN / BR.3
10'-2"
x
11'-8"

BEDRM.2
10'-2"
x
11'-8"

GARAGE
21'-8" x 21'-4"

BRKFST.
SLOPE
10'-0" x 9'-0"

UP

PORCH

46'-0"

70'-0"

Wide-Open and Convenient

No. 20100

Stacked windows fill the wall in the front bedroom of this one-level home, creating an attractive facade, and a sunny atmosphere inside. Around the corner, two more bedrooms and two full baths complete the bedroom wing, set apart for bedtime quiet. Notice the elegant vaulted ceiling in the master bedroom, the master tub and shower illuminated by a skylight, and the double vanities in both baths. Active areas enjoy a spacious feeling. Look at the high, sloping ceilings in the fireplaced living room, the sliders that unite the breakfast room and kitchen with an adjoining deck, and the vaulted ceilings in the formal dining room off the foyer.

Main floor — 1,727 sq. ft.
Basement — 1,727 sq. ft.
Garage — 484 sq. ft.

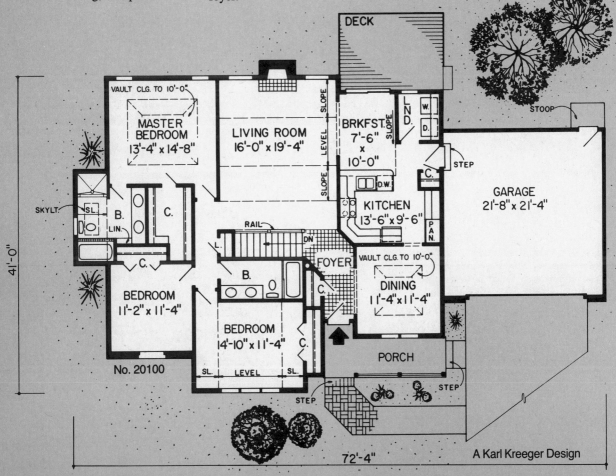

A Karl Kreeger Design

Dramatic Shape and Features

No. 10274

If your lot is the right shape, build this magnificent plan. A dramatically positioned fireplace forms the focus of a contemporary living area. Kitchen, dining, and living spaces are fashioned into a huge central room that flows from the heart of the home through sliding doors to the dramatic deck. The many flexible decorating options, such as screens and room dividers or conversational groupings, are impressive. A huge master bedroom and two roomy bedrooms are tucked in a wing away from the main area for privacy. This home is built on a slab foundation.
Garage — 576 sq. ft.

Total living area — 1,783 sq. ft.

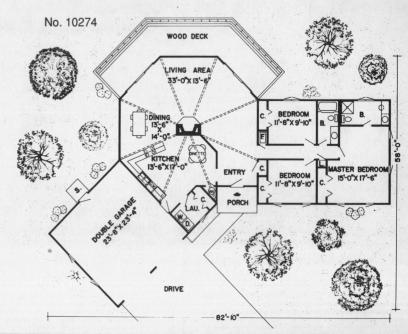

No. 10274

Roofed Walkway Attaches Garage

No. 9181

Placed behind the home and separate, so as not to detract from the rich traditional facade, the garage in this Colonial plan is attached by a roofed walkway. Brick and white pillars grace the exterior, while the interior floor plan speaks of modern luxury. The formal living room and dining room are placed to the left of the foyer, with the family room behind the living room having access to the terrace. To the right of the foyer are three bedrooms, one with a private bathroom.

Living area — 2,014 sq. ft.
Garage — 576 sq. ft.

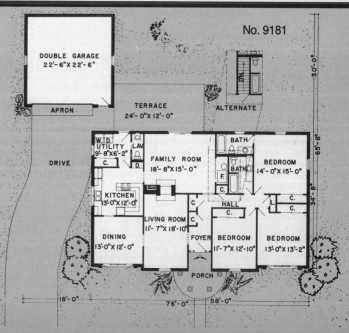

No. 9181

Rustic Ranch with Country Charm

No. 9076

Vacation in rustic comfort. Natural wood siding and a stone chimney highlight the charm of this plan. Sit back on the roomy front porch and enjoy old fashioned peace and quiet. And inside, where the fireplace lights the living and dining rooms, enjoy modern conveniences like the efficient kitchen, roomy closets, and enough bathrooms for a houseful of guests. The main floor of the house is designed compactly so that a retired couple faces a minimum of upkeep. Yet the additional bedrooms offer plenty of room for company. Notice that the bedrooms close off tightly to conserve heating bills. This home can be built on a slab foundation.

First floor — 1,140 sq. ft.
Basement — 1,140 sq. ft.

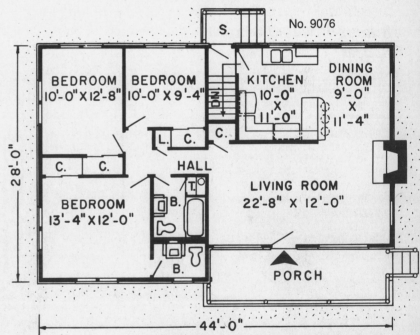

No. 9076

BEDROOM
10'-0" X 12'-8"

BEDROOM
10'-0" X 9'-4"

KITCHEN
10'-0" X 11'-0"

DINING ROOM
9'-0" X 11'-4"

S.

DN

L. C.

C.

C.

HALL

BEDROOM
13'-4" X 12'-0"

B.

T.

LIVING ROOM
22'-8" X 12'-0"

B.

PORCH

28'-0"

44'-0"

Railing Divides Living Spaces

No. 10596

This one-level design is a celebration of light and open space. From the foyer, view the dining room, island kitchen, breakfast room, living room, and outdoor deck in one sweeping glance. Bay windows add pleasing angles and lots of sunshine to eating areas and the master suite. And, a wall of windows brings the outdoors into the two back bedrooms.

Basement — 1,377 sq. ft.

Garage — 480 sq. ft.

Total living area — 1,740 sq. ft.

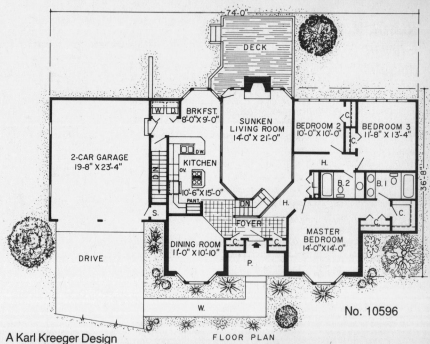

A Karl Kreeger Design

FLOOR PLAN

No. 10596

Ranch Style Favors Living Room

No. 6360

Stretching over 22 feet to span the width of this ranch design, the living room enjoys expanses of windows, a wood-burning fireplace, and access to the terrace. A separate dining room with plenty of windows and an efficient kitchen with abundant counter space border the living room.

House — 1,293 sq. ft.

Basement — 767 sq. ft.

Garage — 466 sq. ft.

Terrace — 92 sq. ft.

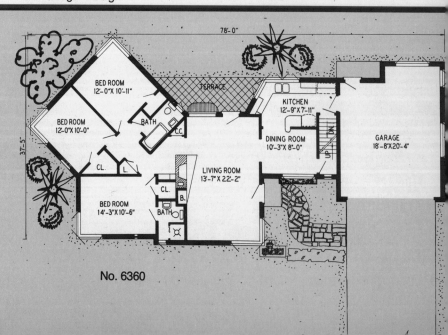

No. 6360

Simple Lines Enhanced by Elegant Window Treatment

No. 10503

Consider this plan if you work at home and would enjoy a homey, well lit office or den. The huge, arched window floods the front room with light. This house offers a lot of other practical details for the two-career family. Compact and efficient use of space means less to clean and organize. Yet the open plan keeps the home from feeling too small and cramped. Other features like plenty of closet space, step-saving laundry facilities, easily-cleaned kitchen, and window wall in the living room make this a delightful plan.

First floor — 1,486 sq. ft.
Basement — 1,486 sq. ft.
Garage — 462 sq. ft.

Total living area — 1,486 sq. ft.

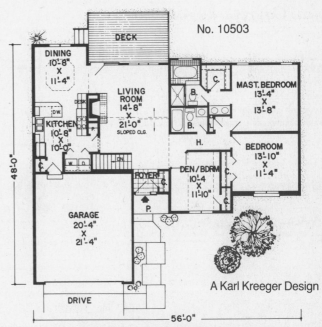

No. 10503

A Karl Kreeger Design

Central Courtyard Features Pool

No. 10507

Created for gracious living, this design is organized around a central courtyard complete with pool. Secluded near one corner of the courtyard, the master bedroom suite is accented by a skylight, spacious walk-in closet, and a bath which accommodates swimmers and sunbathers. The living room, dining room and kitchen occupy another corner. The well-placed kitchen easily serves the patio for comfortable outdoor entertaining. The family room and two more bedrooms complete the design.

First floor — 2,194 sq. ft.
Garage — 576 sq. ft.

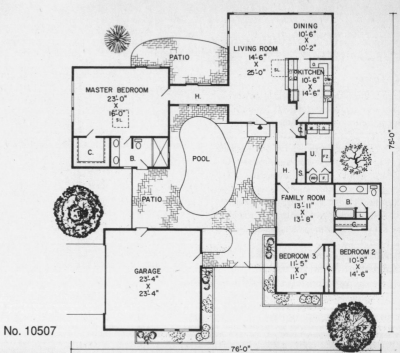

No. 10507

Vacation Retreat Or Year Round Living

No. 1078

A long central hallway divides formal from informal areas, assuring privacy for the two bedrooms located in the rear. Also located along the central portion of the design are a utility room and neighboring bath. The furnace, water heater and washer dryer units are housed in the utility room. An open living/dining room area with exposed beams, sloping ceilings and optional fireplace occupies the design's front. Two pairs of sliding glass doors access the 411 feet of deck from this area. The house may also be entered from the carport on the right or the deck on the left.

First floor – 1,024 sq. ft.
Carport & Storage – 387 sq. ft.
Deck – 411 sq. ft.

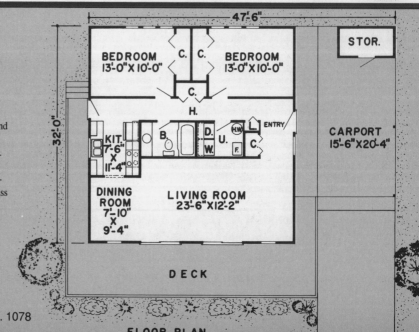

No. 1078

Brick Design has Striking Exterior

No. 10549

This ranch has a circlehead window that sets off a striking exterior view. Inside this single-story design, three bedrooms are located in one part of the plan with all of the bedrooms having separate full baths. The master bedroom features a sloping ceiling, large closet space plus a private bath with both a tub and a shower. Another striking design feature is the great room with its impressive open beams that crisscross down a sloping ceiling. It also has a wood-burning fireplace. The great room also has easy access through sliding glass doors onto an elevated wooden deck. The kitchen leads readily to both the dining and the breakfast rooms. Both of these rooms have decorative ceilings. A half bath lies just off the kitchen as does the utility room.

First floor — 2,280 sq. ft.
Basement — 2,280 sq ft.
Garage — 528 sq. ft.

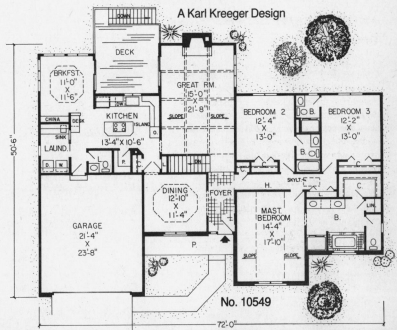

A Karl Kreeger Design

No. 10549

Superior Comfort and Privacy

No. 9828

Consider this refreshing design if you strive for the best. From the beautiful exterior of natural stone to the authentic slate floors in the foyer to the private patio off the master bedroom, this home demonstrates class. You'll appreciate fine touches like the two-way fireplace in between the living room and family room, the magnificent terrace, and the generous dimensions of the rooms. The breakfast nook enjoys a splendid view of the pool through a large bow window. Note the separate terrace entrances, including a mudroom. Four bedrooms are grouped in a wing for privacy, while the maid's room is discretely placed. It can be built on a slab foundation.

Basement — 2,679 sq. ft.
Garage — 541 sq. ft.

Total living area — 2,679 sq. ft.

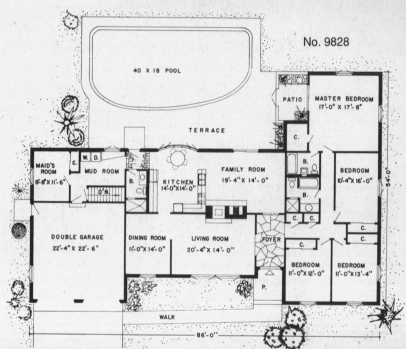

No. 9828

Courtyard Adds Interest

No. 22010

Well-defined contemporary lines are softened by a semi-enclosed courtyard visible from the dining area of this striking design. The 30-foot family room is dominated by a fireplace, resulting in a spacious but cozy area for entertaining. The island kitchen merges with dining nook, and bedrooms are large, featuring the master bedroom and its luxurious bath.

Living area — 2,174 sq. ft.
Garage — 506 sq. ft.

No. 22010

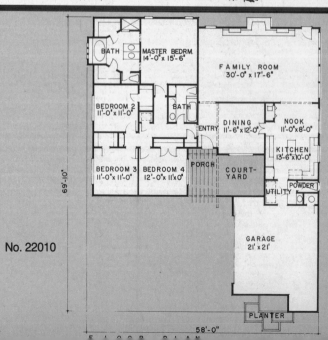

Elegant Entrance to Impressive Home

No. 20057

Two copper-roofed bay windows and a stone veneer front create an elegant entrance through an attractive circle head transom. Enjoy the vaulted ceilings that extend into the foyer, dining room, breakfast room, and master bedroom (with private dressing area). Even the kitchen is impressive with two separate eating areas and a connecting pantry for storage. Sliding glass doors from the breakfast room lead to a huge deck.

Basement — 1,804 sq. ft.
Garage & workshop — 499 sq. ft.

Total living area — 1,804 sq. ft.

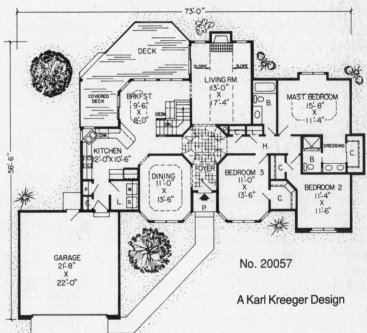

No. 20057

A Karl Kreeger Design

Morning Room Adds Gracious Accent

No. 10445

Tiled floors unify the dining and food preparation areas of this masterful design. Located off the well-organized kitchen is a morning room that's perfect for an elegant brunch or some private time before the day begins. Highlighted by a solarium, this octagonal room opens onto the centrally-located living room that features built-in bookcases, a fireplace, and a wetbar. The family room design employs more tile accents and opens onto the patio. The secluded master bedroom suite features a sunken tub, a small greenhouse for the plant enthusiast, and roomy closets. This plan is built on a slab foundation. Garage — 482 sq. ft.

Total living area — 2,466 sq. ft.

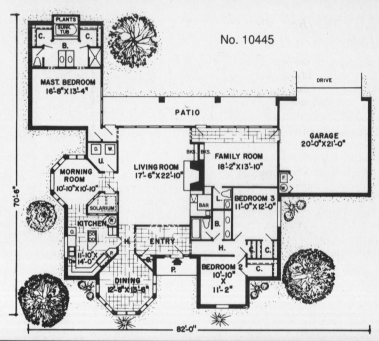

Living, Family Rooms Angled For View

No. 9107

Framed by a redwood balcony, this natural stone and shake shingle design sets living room and family-dining room on an angle and indulges them with windows to capture the view. Sliding glass doors open both rooms to the balcony, and a wood-burning fireplace further equips the family room. Quick meals are possible in the large kitchen, which also allots laundry space. Closeted foyer presents a gracious entrance and all but eliminates cross-traffic through rooms. Four bedrooms and two compartmented baths provide ample sleeping quarters.

First floor – 2,051 sq. ft.
Basement – 1,380 sq. ft.
Garage – 671 sq. ft.

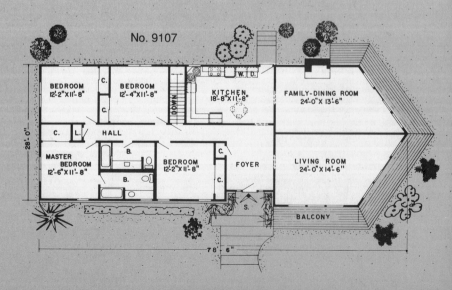

A Karl Kreeger Design

Options Abound

No. 20061

This striking exterior features vertical siding, shake shingles, and rock, to set off a large picture window. Inside, the kitchen has a built-in pantry, refrigerator, dishwasher and range, breakfast bar, an open-beamed ceiling with a skylight, plus a breakfast area with lots of windows. A formal dining room complements the living room, which has two open beams running down a sloping ceiling and a wood-burning fireplace. There is a laundry closet, and the foyer area also has a closet. Three bedrooms share a full bath. The master bedroom has an open-beamed, sloping ceiling with a spacious bath area and a walk-in closet.

Basement — 1,656 sq. ft.
Garage — 472 sq. ft.

Total living area — 1,667 sq. ft.

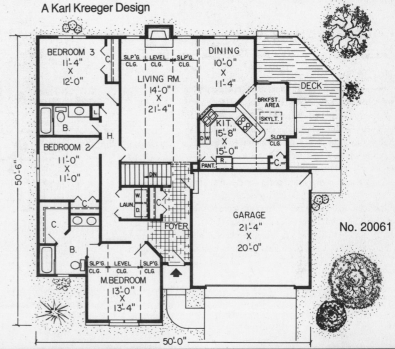

BEDROOM 3
11'-4" X 12'-0"

LIVING RM.
14'-0" X 21'-4"

DINING
10'-0" X 11'-4"

DECK

BRKFST. AREA

KIT.
15'-8" X 15'-0"

SKYLT.

SLOPE CLG.

BEDROOM 2
11'-0" X 11'-0"

50'-6"

LAUN.

PANT.

FOYER

GARAGE
21'-4" X 20'-0"

No. 20061

M.BEDROOM
13'-4" X 13'-4"

50'-0"

Contemporary Ranch Design

No. 26740

Sloping cathedral ceilings are found throughout the entirety of this home. A kitchen holds the central spot in the floor plan. It is partially open to a great hall with firebox and deck access on one side, daylight room lit by ceiling glass and full length windows on another, and entryway hallway on a third. The daylight room leads out onto a unique double deck. Bedrooms lie to the outside of the plan. Two smaller bedrooms at the rear share a full bath. The more secluded master bedroom at the front has its own full bath and access to a private deck.

Living area — 1,512 sq. ft.
Garage — 478 sq. ft.

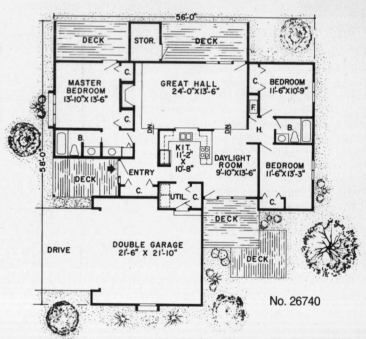

Brick, Diamond Windows Blend Perfectly

No. 9360

This well-designed French Provincial is a beautiful home. The brick, diamond windows, cupola, shutters and color scheme all blend together perfectly. The floor plan is equally desirable. Three bedrooms are served by two full baths, and there is a half-bath combined with the laundry next to the family room. Sliding glass doors in the family room open onto a patio at the rear.

Basement — 2,063 sq. ft.
Garage — 517 sq. ft.

Total living area — 2,055 sq. ft.

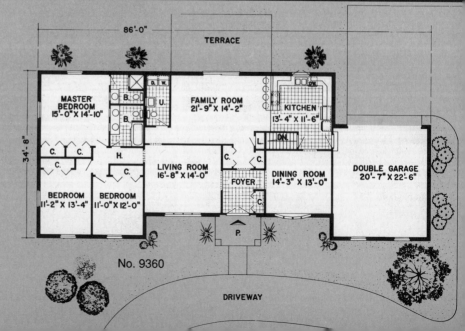

Sunlight Streams Into Many Windows

No. 10456

Twelve-foot beamed ceilings grace the expansive living room with its facing window wall. The adjoining dining room is defined by a lower ceiling and enhanced by an over-sized bay window of leaded glass. The spacious kitchen features many cabinets, a walk-in pantry, center work-island, and a nook overlooking the patio. The master bedroom has a five-piece bath with a skylight, plus an extra large walk-in closet. The two smaller bedrooms share a full bath. A third bedroom located between the kitchen and dining room might find use as a guest bedroom or study. This plan is built on a slab foundation.

Garage — 517 sq. ft.

Total living area — 2,511 sq. ft.

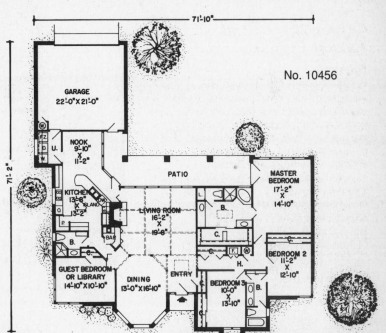

No. 10456

GARAGE
22'-0" X 21'-0"

NOOK
9'-10"
X
11'-2"

PATIO

MASTER
BEDROOM
17'-2"
X
14'-10"

KITCHEN
13'-8"
X ISLAND
13'-2"

LIVING ROOM
16'-2"
X
19'-6"

BAR

BEDROOM 2
11'-2"
X
12'-10"

GUEST BEDROOM
OR LIBRARY
14'-10" X 10'-10"

DINING
13'-0" X 16'-10"

ENTRY

BEDROOM 3
10'-0"
X
13'-10"

71'-10"

71'-2"

Exterior Promise of Luxury Fulfilled

No. 9998

Graceful Spanish arches and stately brick suggests the right attention to detail that is found inside this expansive three bedroom home. The plush master bedroom suite, a prime example, luxuriates in a lounge, a walk-in closet and a private bath. Exposed rustic beams and a cathedral ceiling heightens the formal living room, and an unusually large family room savors a wood-burning fireplace. In addition to the formal dining room, a kitchen with dinette and access to the terrace is planned.

Basement — 2,333 sq. ft.
Garage — 559 sq. ft.

Total living area — 2,333 sq. ft.

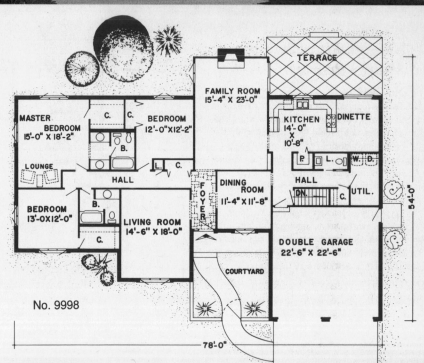

No. 9998

Fireplace Inspires Romantic Dining

No. 9908

Pleasurable dining in the expansive living/dining area is created by the atmospheric wood-burning fireplace in this brick-layered traditional. A functional breakfast bar joins the kitchen and family room, which is placed to enjoy the terrace. A gracious foyer eliminates cross-traffic and allows access to the living or sleeping wing, where three sizable bedrooms and two full baths are provided. The double garage also opens to the terrace.

Main floor — 1,896 sq. ft.
Basement — 1,896 sq. ft.
Garage — 509 sq. ft.

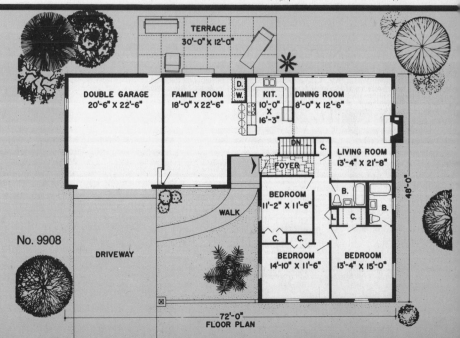

No. 9908

Bedrooms Flank Active Areas for Privacy

No. 20104

Hate to climb stairs? This one-level gem will accommodate your family in style, and keep your housework to a minimum. Recessed ceilings add an elegant touch to the dining room and master suite. And, with half walls, skylights, and a handy rear deck off the sunny breakfast room, there's an airy feeling throughout the centrally-located active areas. You'll appreciate the convenience of built-in storage in the kitchen and fireplaced living room, and the huge bedroom closets that keep the clutter down. Look at the private master bath with its twin vanities, raised tub and walk-in shower. Don't you deserve a little luxury?

Main living area — 1,686 sq. ft.
Basement — 1,677 sq. ft.
Garage — 475 sq. ft.

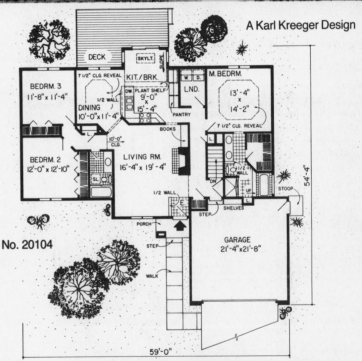

A Karl Kreeger Design

No. 20104

Fireplace In Living and Family Room

No. 9263

This beautiful ranch design features an extra large living room with plenty of formal dining space at the opposite end. Large wood-burning fireplaces are found in both the living and family rooms. A mud room, located off the kitchen, features a laundry area, half bath, and storage closet. The charming master bedroom has a full bath and plenty of closet space.

First floor — 1,878 sq. ft.
Garage — 538 sq. ft.

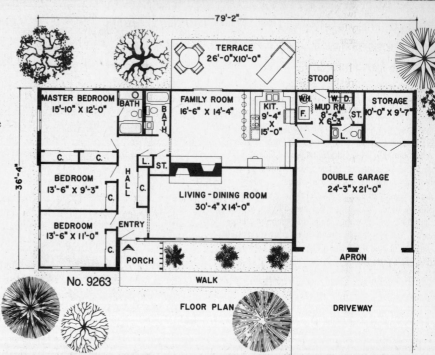

79'-2"

TERRACE 26'-0"X10'-0"

STOOP

MASTER BEDROOM 15'-10" X 12'-0"

BATH

BATH

FAMILY ROOM 16'-6" X 14'-4"

KIT. 9'-4" X 15'-0"

W.H. F.

W. D.

MUD RM. 8'-4" X 6'-3"

STORAGE 0'-0" X 9'-7"

ST.

L.

36'-4"

C. C.

BEDROOM 13'-6" X 9'-3"

HALL

L. ST.

C.

C.

LIVING - DINING ROOM 30'-4" X 14'-0"

DOUBLE GARAGE 24'-3" X 21'-0"

BEDROOM 13'-6" X 11'-0"

ENTRY

C.

PORCH

APRON

No. 9263

WALK

FLOOR PLAN

DRIVEWAY

Bedrooms Enjoy Access to Deck

No. 10220

To encourage a relaxed lifestyle and enjoyment of the outdoors, a 50 foot wooden deck fronts this vacation retreat and opens to two bedrooms as well as the living area. Complete but simple, the plan offers a living area with two closets and a prefab fireplace, open to a compact kitchen with rear entrance. The separate laundry room also houses the furnace and water heater, and the large bath features double sinks. The plan can be built without one or both bedrooms if desired. This plan is built on a crawlspace foundation.

Family area — 576 sq. ft.
Bedroom 1 — 168 sq. ft.
Bedroom 2 — 144 sq. ft.

Total living area — 888 sq. ft.

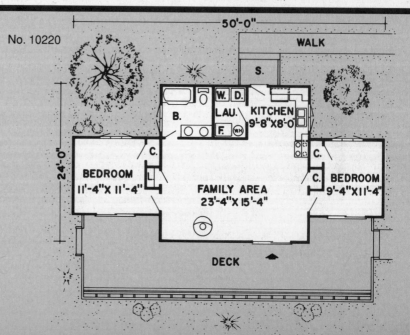

No. 10220

50'-0"

WALK

S.

W. D.

LAU.

KITCHEN 9'-8"X8'-0"

B.

F. WH

24'-0"

C.

C.

BEDROOM 11'-4" X 11'-4"

L

FAMILY AREA 23'-4" X 15'-4"

C.

BEDROOM 9'-4"X11'-4"

DECK

One-Floor Living, Tudor Style

No. 20099

You'll find an appealing quality of open space in every room of this unique one-level home. Angular windows and recessed ceilings separate the two dining rooms from the adjoining island kitchen without compromising the airy feeling. A window-wall that flanks the fireplace in the soaring, skylit living room unites interior spaces with the outdoor deck. The sunny atmosphere continues in the master suite, with its bump-out window and double-vanitied bath, and in the two bedrooms off the foyer. .

Basement — 2,020 sq. ft.
Garage — 534 sq. ft.

Total living area — 2,020 sq. ft.

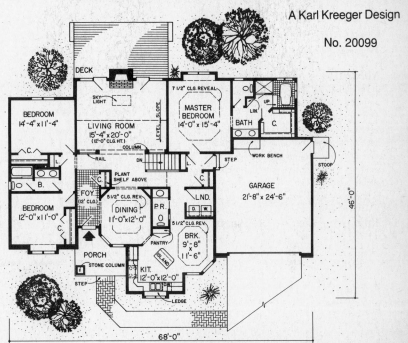

A Karl Kreeger Design

No. 20099

Charming Traditional Emphasizes Living Areas

No. 22014

In addition to its 20 ft. family room with fireplace, this one-story traditional calls for a dining room, breakfast nook, and gameroom that can function as a formal living room if preferred. Each of the three bedrooms adjoins a full bath, with a master bedroom meriting a luxurious "his and hers" bath with two walk-in closets. This plan is built on a slab foundation.

Garage — 485 sq. ft.

Total living area — 2,157 sq. ft.

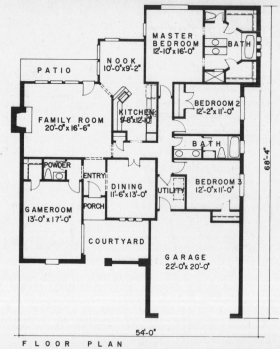

No. 22014

FLOOR PLAN

Berm Design Combines Good Looks with Energy Efficiency

No. 10498

Warmed by earthen walls on three sides, this simple yet elegant design uses an open floor plan to integrate the family living areas and further enhance the energy efficient aspects of this compact home plan. Blended into one living space are the U-shaped kitchen, with its direct access to both the garage and laundry, plus the dining and living rooms. A hearthed fireplace plus built-in bookcases highlight these living areas. A short hall leads to the three bedrooms, each with a south-facing window for additional passive solar gain. Two baths and spacious closets complete the sleeping quarters of this compact design. The foundation of this home is designed for earth berm construction.

Garage — 476 sq. ft.

A Karl Kreeger Design

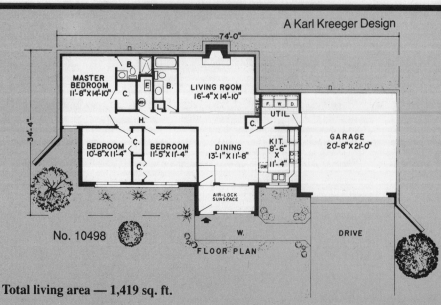

No. 10498

FLOOR PLAN

Total living area — 1,419 sq. ft.

Carefree Living on One Level

No. 20089

Here's an inviting little charmer that will keep housework to a minimum and give you plenty of room for hobbies. A full basement and oversized two-car garage is large enough to store your cars and boat, with space left for a workshop. Upstairs, one-level living is a breeze in this plan that keeps active and quiet areas separate. Three bedrooms and two full baths tucked down a hallway include the spacious master suite with double vanities. The fireplaced living room, dining room, and kitchen are wide open and conveniently arranged for easy mealtimes. Take it easy after dinner, and enjoy dessert and coffee outside on the deck off the dining room.

Main living area — 1,588 sq. ft.
Basement — 780 sq. ft.
Garage — 808 sq. ft.

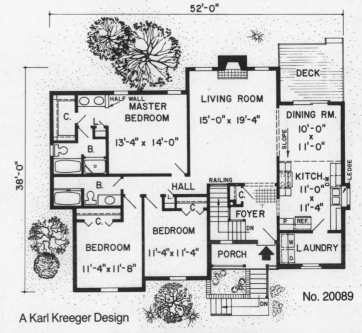

A Karl Kreeger Design

No. 20089

Ranch Design
Utilizes Skylights

No. 10570

A partial stone veneer front makes this large ranch design very inviting. Inside, a vestibule entry serves as an airtight air-lock. A large library/den next to the foyer shares a two-way fireplace with the living room and has a sloped ceiling, as does the living room. The living room leads to a deck or screened porch. A very large kitchen has a hexagonal island with a connecting dining room. The dining room also has skylights, adding warmth and additional lighting to the room. Also in the dining room, sliding glass doors lead out to the veranda. This spacious design has four bedrooms and ample closet space.

Main floor — 2,450 sq. ft.
Basement — 2,450 sq. ft.
Garage — 739 sq. ft.

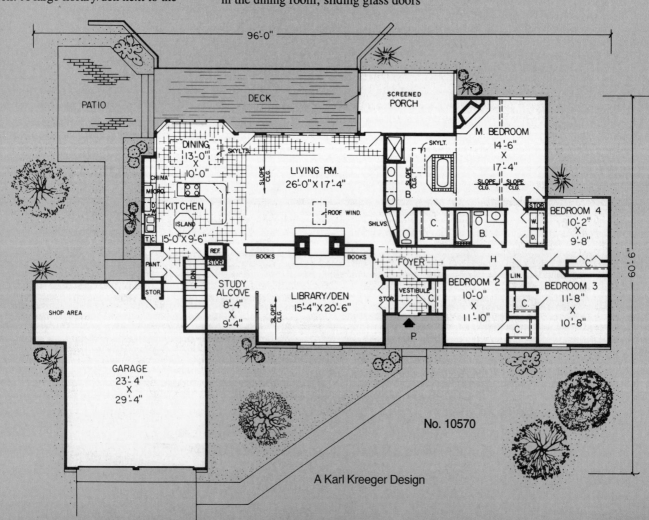

No. 10570

A Karl Kreeger Design

Colonial Detailing Enlivens Exterior

No. 10020

Impressive Colonial columns punctuate the semi-circular porch and fuse with the bow windows and brick to create an exceptional facade. Inside, the floor plan is a study in the modern living. Fireplaces grace both the living room and the family room, which opens to an expansive terrace. A formal dining room adjoins the highly functional kitchen, and the 21-foot master bedroom boasts a lavish full bath and double closets. Two front bedrooms are accented with lovely bow windows.

First floor — 2,512 sq. ft.
Basement — 2,512 sq. ft.
Garage — 648 sq. ft.

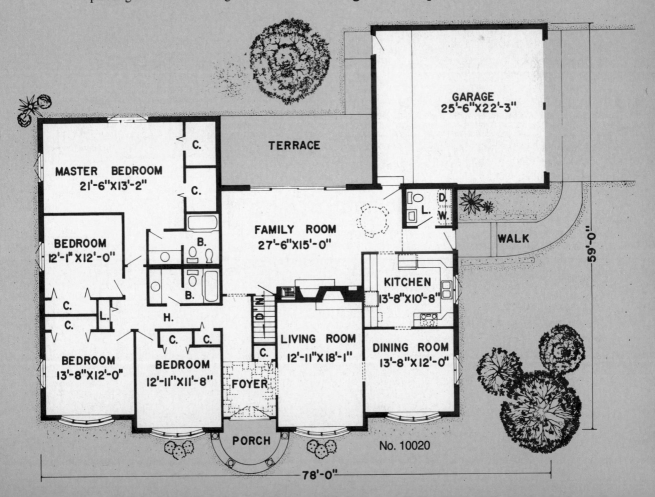

No. 10020

Secluded and Spectacular Bedroom

No. 10451

Create a secluded sanctuary for your master bedroom: a generous space with charming fireplace, individual dressing rooms, and skylit bathing area. Relax away from the clutter and noise of the children's rooms, especially if you create a study or sewing room from bedroom two. You'll love the courtyard effect created by glassed-in living spaces overlooking the central covered patio with skylights. The sprawling charm of this house creates a sense of privacy everywhere you go. Extra touches, such as the wetbar and dual fireplaces for family and living room set this home apart. This plan is built on a slab foundation.

Garage — 607 sq. ft.

Total living area — 2,864 sq. ft.

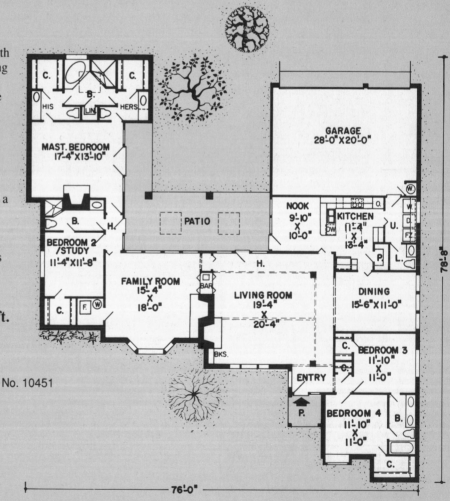

No. 10451

Master Bedroom Merits Deck

No. 10270

Consider this home for the family with hobbies. With plenty of living space in an easy-to-clean single level design and accommodations for a workshop and outdoor activities, this design is perfectly practical. Admire the elegant touches too, like the huge bow windows, the deluxe master bath with corner tub, and two appealing decks. The family kitchen boasts an efficient layout that simplifies daily meals. First-floor laundry facilities save time and steps.

Basement — 2,016 sq. ft.
Garage & workshop — 677 sq. ft.

Total living area — 2,202 sq. ft.

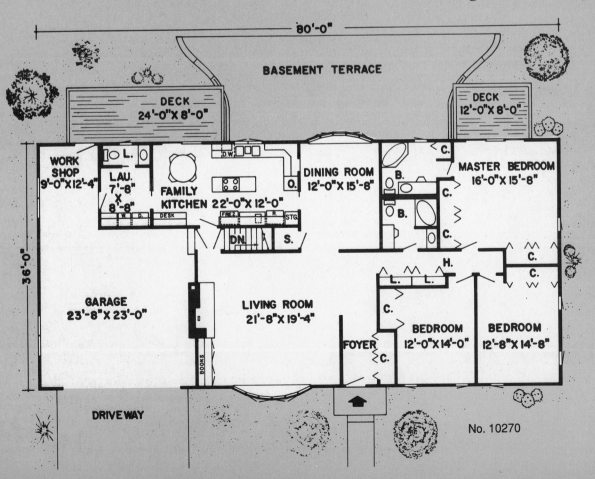

No. 10270

Ranch Incorporates Victorian Features

No. 20058

This wonderful Victorian-featured ranch design incorporates many luxury conveniences usually offered in larger designs. The master bedroom is expansive in size, with an oversized full bath complete with a walk-in closet, an individual shower, a full tub, and a two-sink wash basin. A large kitchen area is offered with a built-in island for convenience. The kitchen also has its own breakfast area. Located next to the kitchen is a half bath. The living area is separated from the dining room by a half-partition wall. Two large bedrooms complete the interior of the house. They have large closets and share a full bath. A two-car garage and a wood deck complete the options listed in this design.

Basement — 1,787 sq. ft.
Garage — 484 sq. ft.

Total living area — 1,787 sq. ft.

A Karl Kreeger Design

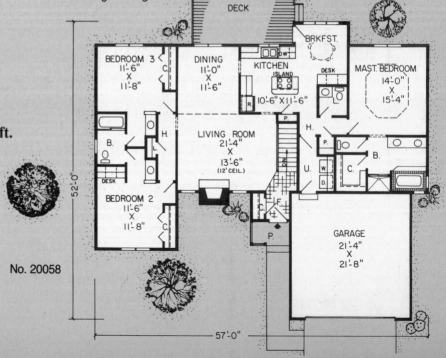

No. 20058

Split Level Home

Fireplace Adds a Cozy Touch

No. 10760

Here's a handsome split-entry home that separates active and quiet areas. Step down to the garage level that includes a basement recreation and workshop area perfect for the household hobbyist. A short staircase leads up to the soaring living room, where the open feeling is accentuated by a huge bow window and a wide opening to the formal dining room. The kitchen lies behind swinging double doors, and features access to a raised rear deck. A few steps up, you'll find two full baths and three bedrooms with extra-large closets. Sloping ceilings add dramatic appeal to the private bedroom wing.

First floor — 1,676 sq. ft.
Basement recreation area — 592 sq. ft.
Workshop — 144 sq. ft.
Garage — 697 sq. ft.

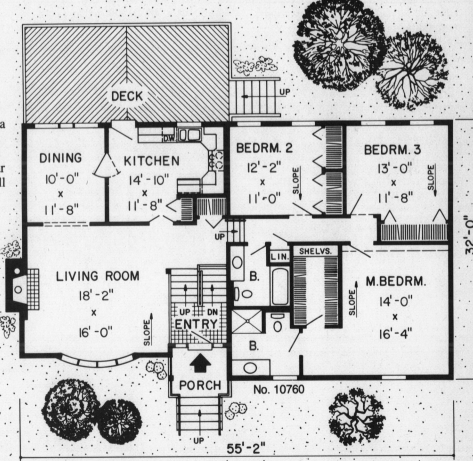

DECK

UP

DINING
10'-0"
x
11'-8"

KITCHEN
14'-10"
x
11'-8"

DW.

BEDRM. 2
12'-2"
x
11'-0"

SLOPE

BEDRM. 3
13'-0"
x
11'-8"

SLOPE

32'-0"

UP

LIN. SHELVS.

LIVING ROOM
18'-2"
x
16'-0"

SLOPE

UP DN
ENTRY

B.

B.

M.BEDRM.
14'-0"
x
16'-4"

SLOPE

PORCH

No. 10760

UP

55'-2"

Enjoy the View

No. 20095

Step into the sunwashed foyer of this contemporary beauty, and you'll be faced with a choice. You can walk downstairs into a huge, fireplaced rec room with built-in bar and adjoining patio.

Three bedrooms and a full bath complete the lower level. Or, you can ascend the stairs to a massive living room with sloping ceilings, a tiled fireplace, and a commanding view of the back yard. Sharing the view, the breakfast nook with sunny bay opens to an outdoor deck. The adjoining kitchen is just steps away from

the formal dining room, which features recessed ceilings and overlooks the foyer You'll also find the master suite on this level, just past the powder room off the living room.

Upper level — 1,448 sq. ft.
Lower level — 1,029 sq. ft.
Garage — 504 sq. ft.

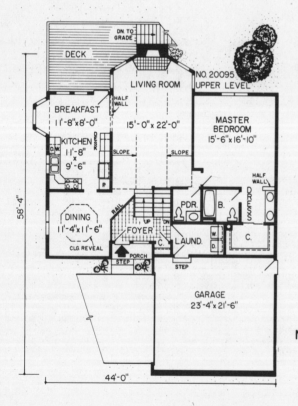

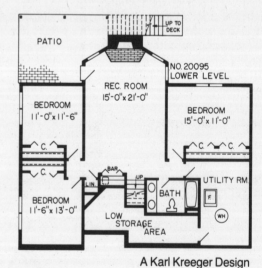

A Karl Kreeger Design

No. 20095

Half-Round Window Graces Attractive Exterior

No. 90395

This handsome home combines convenience and drama by adding a bedroom wing a half-level above active areas. The result of this distinctive design is a striking, spacious feeling in living spaces, along with uncompromised privacy for the two bedrooms at the rear of the house. Look at the soaring ceilings of the kitchen, living, dining, and breakfast rooms. Notice the little touches that make life easier: the private bath entrance from the master suite, the pass-through between kitchen and dining room, the built-in planning desk, the bookcases that flank the fireplace. Don't need a third bedroom? The front room on the entry level doubles as a home office or den.

Main living area — 1,452 sq. ft.
Garage — 2-car

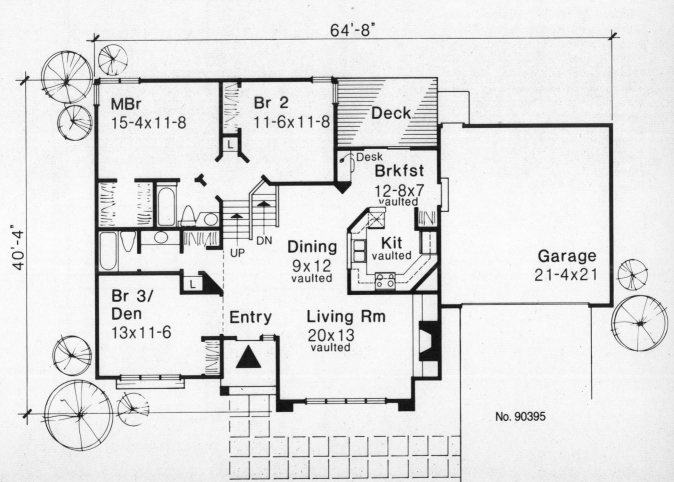

No. 90395

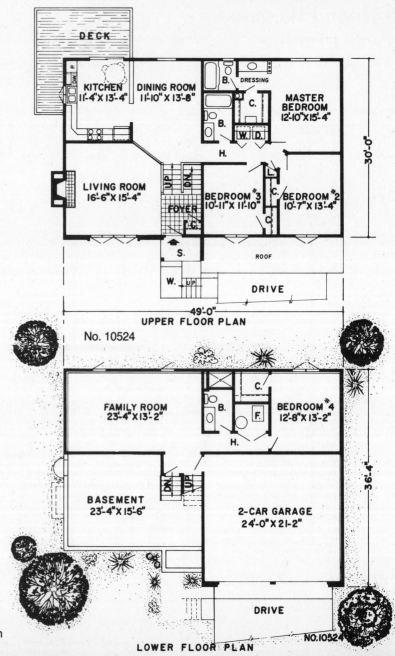

Split-level Made for Growing Family

No. 10524

The entry-level living room features a fireplace and, just a few steps up, a dining room which overlooks the living room and adjoins the kitchen. The efficient kitchen features an eat-in space and sliding-door access to the deck. Three bedrooms, two baths, and a convenient laundry room comprise the rest of the upper floor. The fourth bedroom, with its own bath, could be used as a guest room or to give more privacy to the teenager in the family. There's also a cozy family room and plenty of storage in the basement.

Upper floor — 1,470 sq. ft.
Lower floor — 711 sq. ft.
Basement — 392 sq. ft.
Garage — 563 sq. ft.

A Karl Kreeger Design

Split Level Home

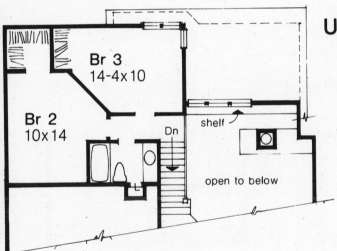

Upper Floor

Br 3
14-4 x 10

Br 2
10 x 14

Dn

shelf

open to below

U-Shaped Kitchen Offers Breakfast Bay Window Area

No. 90372

Perceived value, that sales appealing characteristic that justifies the high cost of a new home in your customer's mind, is strongly featured in this home. The exterior has substantial mass and interest. The interior has lots of impact and volume. Combined, the package also features the master bedroom suite on the main floor, the open U-shaped kitchen with breakfast bay, the vaulted living room with tall wall fireplace focus. The style is very "today", quite contemporary in spirit but very reflective of traditional story and a half homes values of the past.

First floor — 1,006 sq. ft.
Second floor — 437 sq. ft.

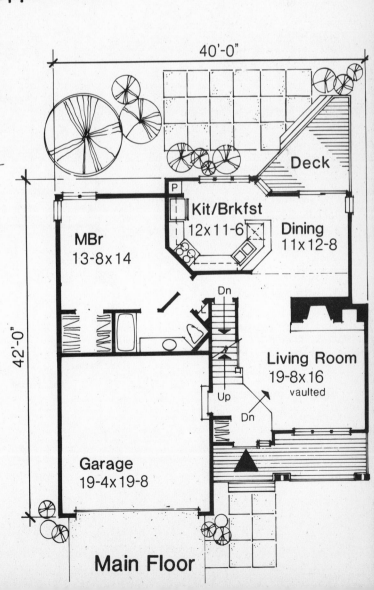

40'-0"

Deck

P

Kit/Brkfst
12 x 11-6

Dining
11 x 12-8

MBr
13-8 x 14

42'-0"

Dn

Living Room
19-8 x 16
vaulted

Up

Dn

Garage
19-4 x 19-8

Main Floor

Traditional Trend-Setter

No. 10776

Watch the world go by from the beautiful, floor-to-ceiling bay window in the cozy living room of this unusual, multi-level home. Active areas sharing the entry level with the fireplaced living room include a formal dining room with sliders to a rear deck. Steps away, the adjoining, well-equipped kitchen features a built-in pantry and planning desk. A half flight of stairs separates this area from the quiet atmosphere of the bedroom wing, a distinctive difference from the traditional ranch, or two-story design. The front-facing bedrooms tucked over the attached, two-car garage share a hall bath. But, the master suite features its own private bath with step-in shower.

First floor — 1,200 sq. ft.
Basement (finished) — 482 sq. ft.
Basement (unfinished) — 548 sq. ft.
Garage — 575 sq. ft.

Total living area —1,682 sq. ft.

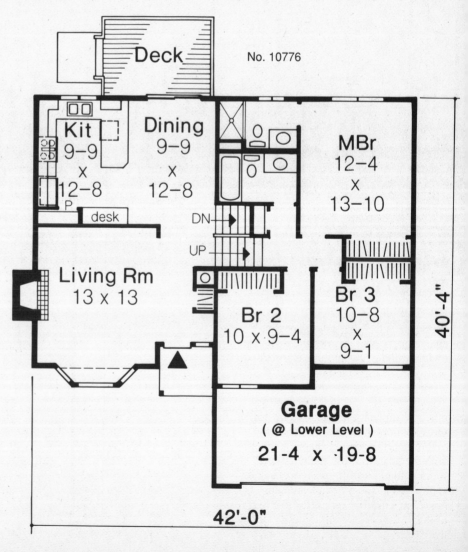

Hillside Haven

No. 20148

Unusual angles add a unique flair to this adaptable charmer. The central foyer features an open railing that sets off the half-stairway to the private master suite. To the right, you'll find a well-appointed kitchen that adjoins a cheerful, six-sided breakfast room with access to the wrap-around deck. The rear-facing dining room is great for formal suppers. And its handy location next to the skylit living room with built-in wetbar will simplify your entertaining duties. Two more bedrooms, tucked down a hall off the living room, share a full bath with double vanities.

Basement — 1,399 sq. ft.
Garage — 551 sq. ft.

Total living area — 1,774 sq. ft.

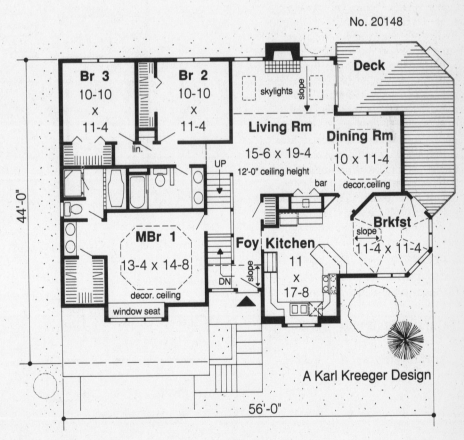

No. 20148

A Karl Kreeger Design

Split Level Home

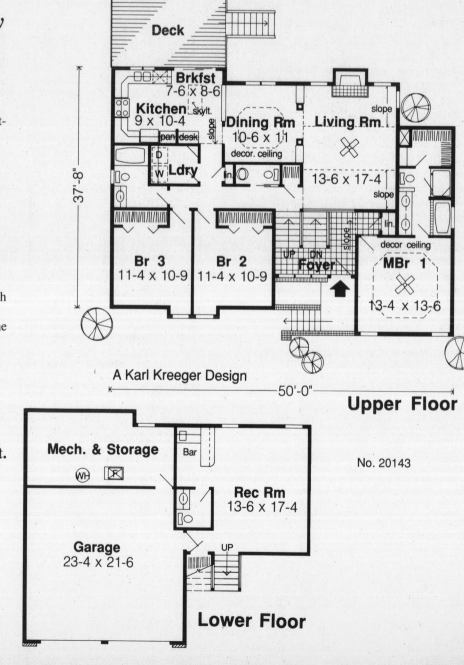

Split Level Home

Stunning Split-Entry

No. 20143

This spacious split-entry home with a contemporary flavor is the perfect answer to the needs of your growing family. Imagine the convenience of a rec room with a built-in bar, powder room, and storage space on the garage level. Picture the luxury of your own, private master suite tucked off the foyer, featuring a walk-in closet, double-vanitied bath, and decorative ceilings. Active areas a few steps up include an expansive, fireplaced living room overlooking the foyer, an adjoining dining room graced with decorative ceilings and columns, and a skylit kitchen and breakfast room loaded with built-in amenities. Two bedrooms over the garage are steps away from the hall bath or the powder room. This plan is built on a combination slab-crawlspace foundation.

Upper floor — 1,599 sq. ft.
Lower floor — 346 sq. ft.
Garage — 520 sq. ft.

Total living area — 1,945 sq. ft.

Deck

Brkfst 7-6 x 8-6

Kitchen 9 x 10-4

pan desk

Dining Rm 10-6 x 11
decor. ceiling

Living Rm
slope
13-6 x 17-4
slope

skylt.
slope

Ldr y
D
W

37'-8"

Br 3 11-4 x 10-9

Br 2 11-4 x 10-9

UP DN **Foyer**
slope

lin.

decor ceiling

MBr 1
13-4 x 13-6

A Karl Kreeger Design

50'-0"

Upper Floor

Mech. & Storage
WH

Bar

Rec Rm 13-6 x 17-4

No. 20143

Garage 23-4 x 21-6

UP

Lower Floor

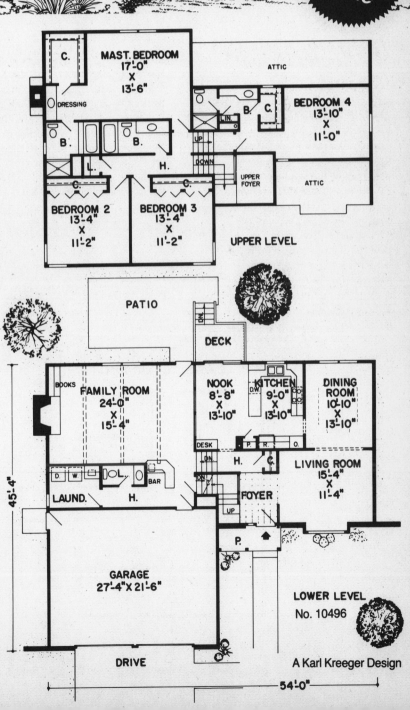

Dignified Design
Opens to Family Style
Floor Plan

No. 10496

Four spacious bedrooms are arranged on the upper level of this plan so that privacy is maintained without any wasted space. Two of the bedrooms share a bath while the other two large bedrooms each have a private bath and a walk-in closet. The living space on the lower level is highlighted by a spacious family room with a beamed ceiling, fireplace, bookcases, wetbar and direct access to both the patio and informal dining nook. The more formal dining room and living room are located on the other side of the well-designed U-shaped kitchen. The double garage even has plenty of room for a workshop and extra bicycles.

Lower level — 1,330 sq. ft.
Upper level — 1,301 sq. ft.
Garage — 610 sq. ft.
Basement — 765 sq. ft.

Split Level Home

MAST. BEDROOM 17'-0" X 13'-6"

ATTIC

BEDROOM 4 13'-10" X 11'-0"

C.

DRESSING

B.

B.

LIN.

B.

C.

UP

DOWN

L.

H.

UPPER FOYER

ATTIC

BEDROOM 2 13'-4" X 11'-2"

BEDROOM 3 13'-4" X 11'-2"

C.

C.

UPPER LEVEL

PATIO

DECK

DN

BOOKS

FAMILY ROOM 24'-0" X 15'-4"

NOOK 8'-8" X 13'-10"

KITCHEN 9'-0" X 13'-10"

D.W.

DINING ROOM 10'-10" X 13'-10"

DESK

P.

R.

O.

DN

H.

C.

LIVING ROOM 15'-4" X 11'-4"

D

W

L.

BAR

LAUND.

H.

DN

FOYER

UP

45'-4"

P.

GARAGE 27'-4" X 21'-6"

LOWER LEVEL
No. 10496

DRIVE

54'-0"

A Karl Kreeger Design

Split Level Home

Perfectly Private

No. 20169

This house offers multi-level living at its best. The elegant dining room off the foyer, with its bay windows and a decorative ceiling, creates a great impression on entering guests. Steps away, you'll find an island kitchen planned for efficiency. A plant shelf crowns the sloping ceilings of the adjoining breakfast room, which features sliding glass doors to a rear deck. Open staircases and huge windows make the large, fireplaced living room seem even more spacious. Step down one staircase to the garage level, or up another to the privacy of the bedroom wing. High, arched windows accent the two front bedrooms, which share the hall bath. The master suite enjoys its own bath and walk-in closet.

Basement — 792 sq. ft.
Garage — 632 sq. ft.

Total living area — 1,472 sq. ft.

Floor Plan

A Karl Kreeger Design

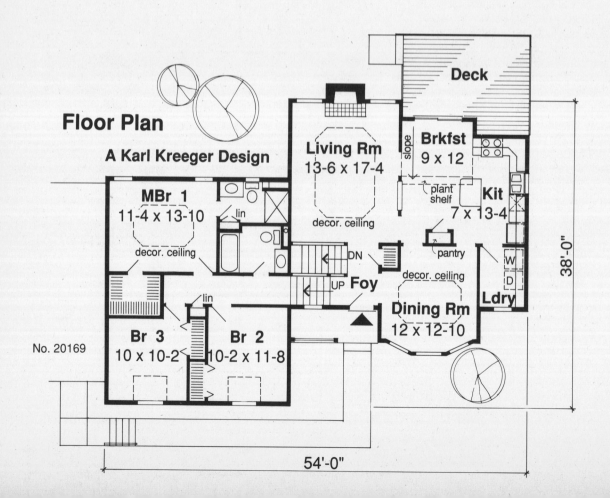

Deck

Living Rm
13-6 x 17-4
decor. ceiling

Brkfst
9 x 12

slope

plant shelf

Kit
7 x 13-4

MBr 1
11-4 x 13-10
decor. ceiling

lin

pantry

W
D

DN

UP Foy

decor. ceiling

Ldry

Br 3
10 x 10-2

lin

Br 2
10-2 x 11-8

Dining Rm
12 x 12-10

No. 20169

38'-0"

54'-0"

Master Suite Crowns Outstanding Plan

No. 10334

Here's a fabulous executive home. Incorporating a study, walk-in closet, and lavish bath with whirlpool, shower, and skylight, the master suite adds a finishing touch to this exceptional home. The deck-edged main level details an eye-catching 25-ft. oak floored great room with bow window. Also outlined are two bedrooms, a slate floored dining room, and kitchen with pantry and snack island. On the basement level, the family room joins the patio via sliding glass doors, and a fourth bedroom and extra bath are included.

Main level — 1,742 sq. ft.
Upper level — 809 sq. ft.
Lower level — 443 sq. ft.
Basement — 1,270 sq. ft.
Garage — 558 sq. ft.

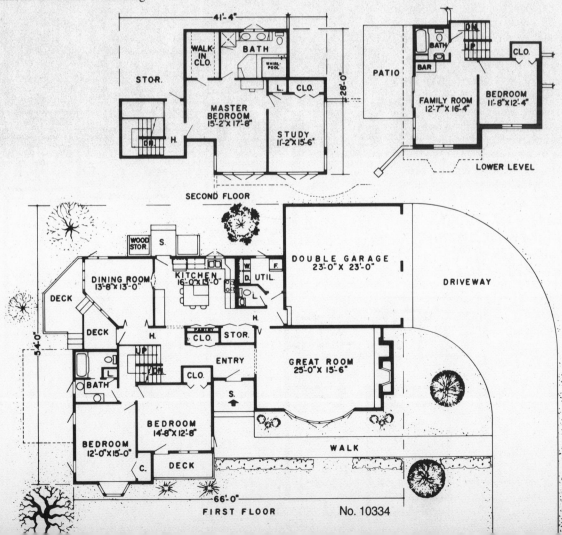

FIRST FLOOR   No. 10334

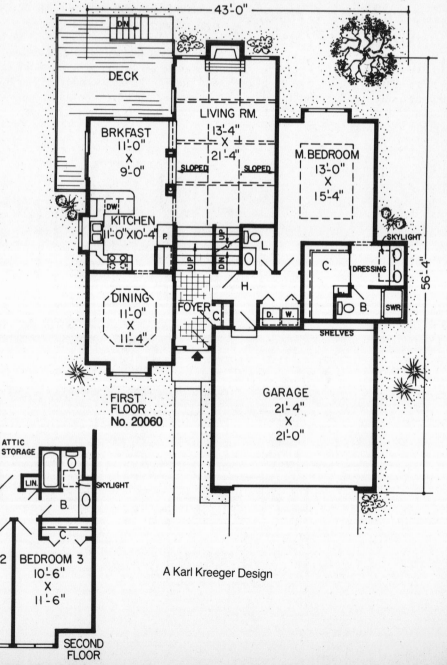

Split Level Home

Master Bedroom at Entry Level

No. 20060

Striking angles best describes this contemporary design. At the front entrance, an attractive half-circle window transom is built above the door. Through the foyer, the kitchen is centered perfectly between the breakfast area and a more formal dining area. The breakfast room leads onto a very large wooden deck through sliding glass doors. From the breakfast room, the living room comes complete with a burning fireplace, plus the extra feature of a sloping, open beamed ceiling. This design offers the master bedroom on the entry level, with a dressing area, walk-in closet, and full bath. The second level offers two bedrooms with a full bath and a convenient cedar closet.

First floor — 1,279 sq. ft.
Second floor — 502 sq. ft.
Basement — 729 sq. ft.
Garage — 470 sq. ft.

DECK

LIVING RM.
13'-4"
X
21'-4"
SLOPED   SLOPED

BRKFAST
11'-0"
X
9'-0"

M. BEDROOM
13'-0"
X
15'-4"

SKYLIGHT

KITCHEN
11'-0"X10'-4"

C.   DRESSING

DW
H.
B.
SWR

DINING
11'-0"
X
11'-4"

FOYER
C.
D. W.
SHELVES

43'-0"

56'-4"

FIRST FLOOR
No. 20060

GARAGE
21'-4"
X
21'-0"

LIVING ROOM

ATTIC STORAGE

CEDAR CLO.

LIN.

SKYLIGHT

H.
B.

SLOPE

C.   C.

BEDROOM 2
10'-6"
X
11'-6"

BEDROOM 3
10'-6"
X
11'-6"

A Karl Kreeger Design

SECOND FLOOR

44

Comfortable Family Room in Congenial Setting

No. 90520

A secluded porch provides an intimate entrance to this 3 bedroom home. You'll appreciate the large family room with fireplace as the center for many activities. The breakfast nook will be popular with its nearby bow window and will be practible near the pantry and kitchen. The dining area also is easy to serve. The living room will have a wonderful view through the bow window. The master bedroom is complete, including dressing area and walk-in wardrobe.

First floor — 1,048 sq. ft.
Second floor — 726 sq. ft.

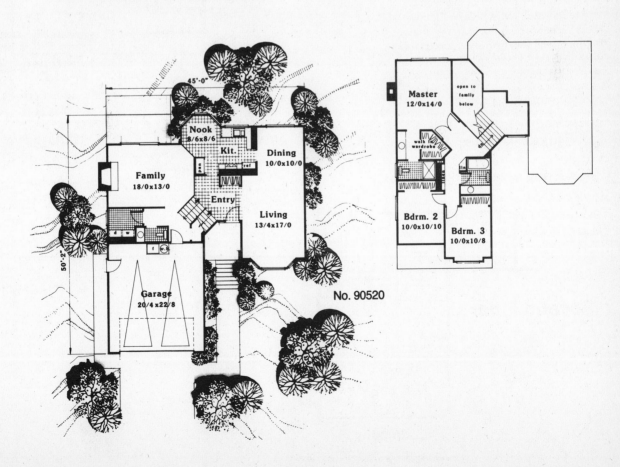

No. 90520

Split Level Home

Home on a Hill

No. 20501

Your hillside lot is no problem if you choose this spectacular, multi-level sun-catcher. Window walls combine with sliders to unite active areas with a huge outdoor deck. Interior spaces flow together for an open feeling that's accentuated by the sloping ceilings and towering fireplace in the living room. Thanks to the island kitchen, even the cook can stay involved in the action. Walk up a short flight to reach the laundry room, a full bath, and two bedrooms, each with a walk-in closet. Up a separate staircase, you'll find the master suite, truly a private retreat complete with a garden spa, abundant closets, and balcony.

First floor — 1,300 sq. ft.
Second floor — 566 sq. ft.

Total living area — 1,866 sq. ft.

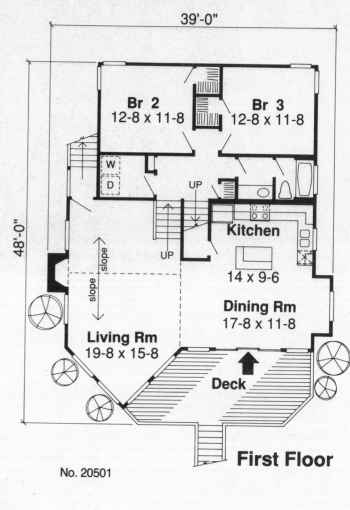

No. 20501

First Floor

39'-0"

48'-0"

Br 2
12-8 x 11-8

Br 3
12-8 x 11-8

W
D

UP

UP

Kitchen

14 x 9-6

Dining Rm
17-8 x 11-8

Living Rm
19-8 x 15-8

Deck

slope

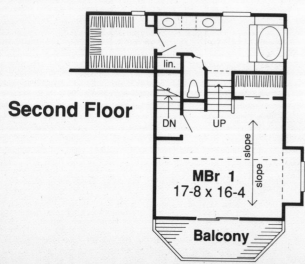

Second Floor

lin.

DN   UP

slope

MBr 1
17-8 x 16-4

Balcony

Family Favorite

No. 20156

The elegant half-round windows flanking the clapboard-faced chimney hint at the comfortable atmosphere you'll find inside this easy-care ranch. An open arrangement with the dining room combines with ten-foot ceilings to make the sunny living room seem even more spacious than its generous size. Glass on three sides overlooking the deck off the dining room adds an outdoor feeling to both rooms. And the compact kitchen, designed for efficiency, is just steps away. You'll appreciate the private location of the bedrooms, tucked away for a quiet atmosphere. The master suite is a special retreat, with its romantic window seat, compartmentalized bath and walk-in closet.

Basement — 1,359 sq. ft.

Garage — 501 sq. ft.

Total living area — 1,359 sq. ft.

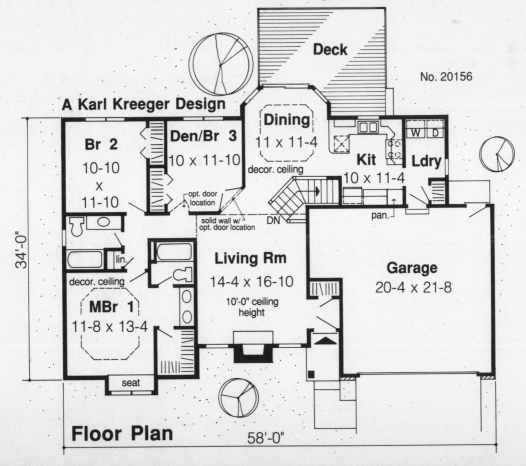

No. 20156

A Karl Kreeger Design

Deck

Dining
11 x 11-4
decor. ceiling

Kit
10 x 11-4

Ldry
W D

Br 2
10-10
x
11-10

Den/Br 3
10 x 11-10

opt. door location

solid wall w/
opt. door location

DN

pan.

lin.

decor. ceiling

MBr 1
11-8 x 13-4

seat

Living Rm
14-4 x 16-10

10'-0" ceiling height

Garage
20-4 x 21-8

34'-0"

58'-0"

Floor Plan

Carefully Designed for Compact Spaces

No. 10771

The amenities featured in this compact, one-level plan prove you don't have to build large to have what you want in a home. Notice the garden wall that insures privacy in the master suite, the two full baths, the attached garage, the built-in wetbar in the fireplaced living room, and the walled patio accessible through sliding glass doors in both dining and living rooms. Look at the mealtime choices you have: informal family suppers and quick snacks in the sunny breakfast nook, or elegant dinners in the spacious dining room overlooking the patio. Other assets of this appealing home include double closets and vanities in the master suite, and the handy laundry corner tucked off the breakfast room.

Main living area — 1,305 sq. ft.
Garage — one-car

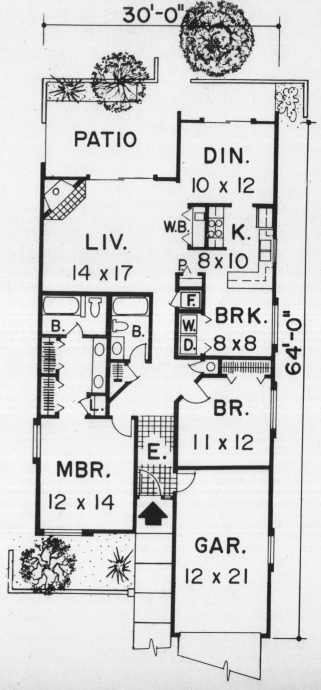

Another Nice Ranch Design

No. 90354

Small and move-up houses are looking much larger these days thanks to clever proportions and roof masses, as exemplified in this two-bedroom ranch. The inside space seems larger, from the high-impact entrance with through-views to the vaulted great room, fireplace, and rear deck. The den (optional third bedroom) features double doors. The kitchen & breakfast area has a vaulted ceiling. The plan easily adapts to crawl or slab construction with utilities replacing stairs, laundry facing the kitchen, and air handler and water heater facing the garage.

Living Area — 1,360 sq. ft.

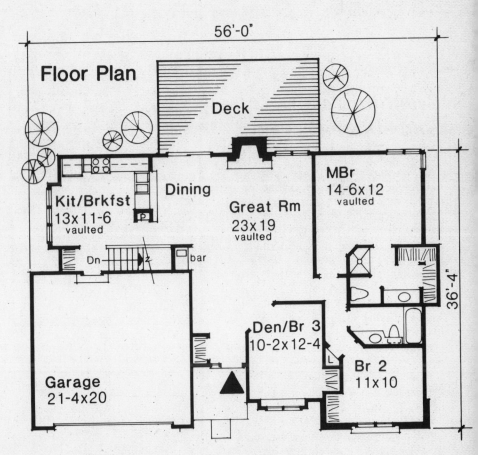

Floor Plan

56'-0"

Deck

Kit/Brkfst
13x11-6
vaulted

Dining

Great Rm
23x19
vaulted

MBr
14-6x12
vaulted

Dn   bar

Garage
21-4x20

Den/Br 3
10-2x12-4

Br 2
11x10

36'-4"

No. 90354

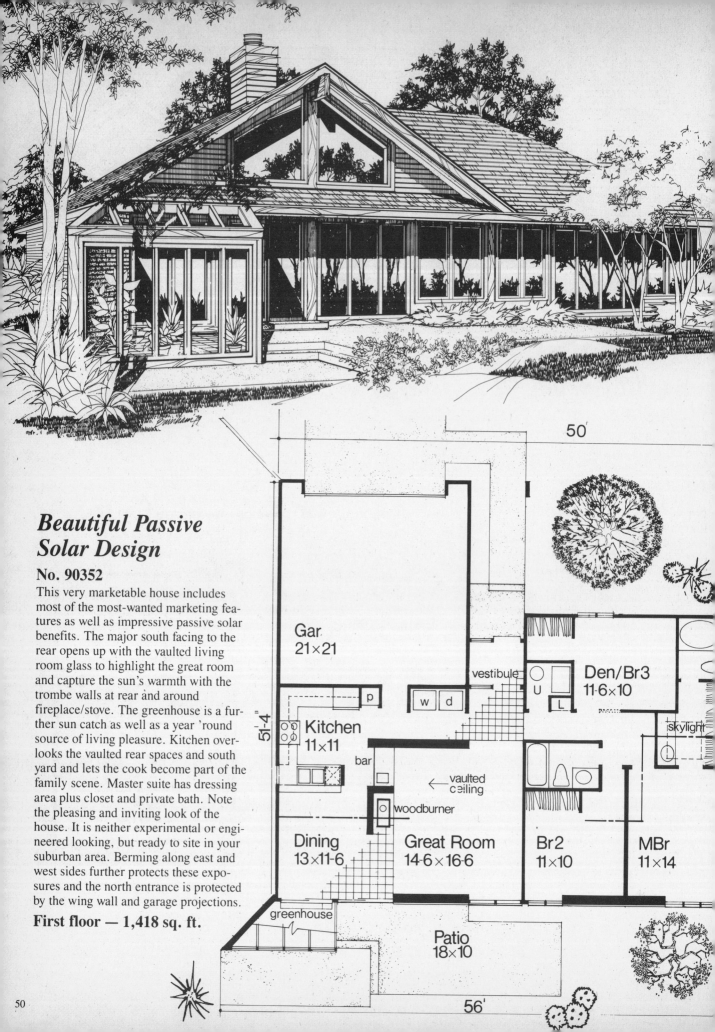

Beautiful Passive Solar Design

No. 90352

This very marketable house includes most of the most-wanted marketing features as well as impressive passive solar benefits. The major south facing to the rear opens up with the vaulted living room glass to highlight the great room and capture the sun's warmth with the trombe walls at rear and around fireplace/stove. The greenhouse is a further sun catch as well as a year 'round source of living pleasure. Kitchen overlooks the vaulted rear spaces and south yard and lets the cook become part of the family scene. Master suite has dressing area plus closet and private bath. Note the pleasing and inviting look of the house. It is neither experimental or engineered looking, but ready to site in your suburban area. Berming along east and west sides further protects these exposures and the north entrance is protected by the wing wall and garage projections.

First floor — 1,418 sq. ft.

50'

51'-4"

Gar.
21×21

vestibule

w   d

Den/Br3
11-6×10

skylight

Kitchen
11×11

p

bar

← vaulted
ceiling

woodburner

Dining
13×11-6

Great Room
14-6×16-6

Br2
11×10

MBr
11×14

greenhouse

Patio
18×10

56'

50

Central Courtyard Creates Appealing Entry

No. 99311

Romance and drama combine in this easy-living home characterized by loads of windows and a wide-open feeling. Standing in the foyer, you'll be amazed at the view before you: the soaring, sunken living room with a massive fireplace flanked by windows and French doors to a rear deck, the efficient kitchen with wetbar pass through to the living room, and the vaulted master suite with its corner window seat. But, the view isn't the only appealing feature of this handsome house. Look at the private, doublevanitied master bath, the elegant, angular dining room with access to a screened porch overlooking the backyard, and the two sunny bedrooms that share a full bath just across the hall.

Main living area — 1,640 sq. ft.
Garage — 2-car

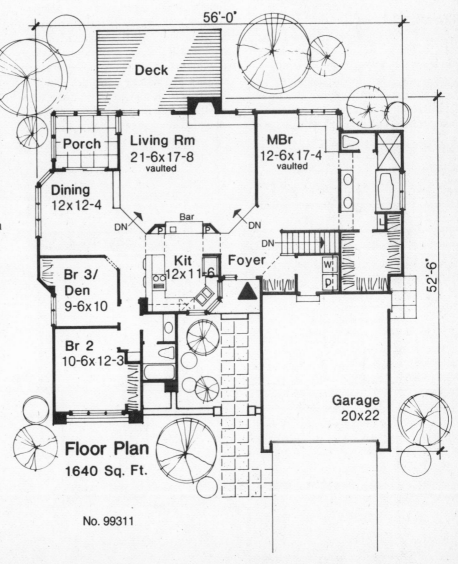

Floor Plan
1640 Sq. Ft.

No. 99311

Covered Porches Add Outdoor Living Space

No. 90247

Step past the walled garden, stand in the entry of this sprawling, one-level home and feast your eyes. In one sweeping glance, you'll see the elegant dining room and parlor, the fireplace that dominates the gathering room, the two covered porches, and the backyard. A hallway dividing the house front to back leads past the study to three bedrooms and two full baths. The master suite features sliders to a private terrace, along with its own bath and dressing room with built-in vanity. At the other end of the hall, you'll find the nook adjoining the island kitchen, which is linked to the formal dining room by the butler's pantry. Handy service and garage entries, close to kitchen storage and utility areas, are an added convenience that make this home even more appealing.

Main living area — 3,225 sq. ft.
Garage — 2-car

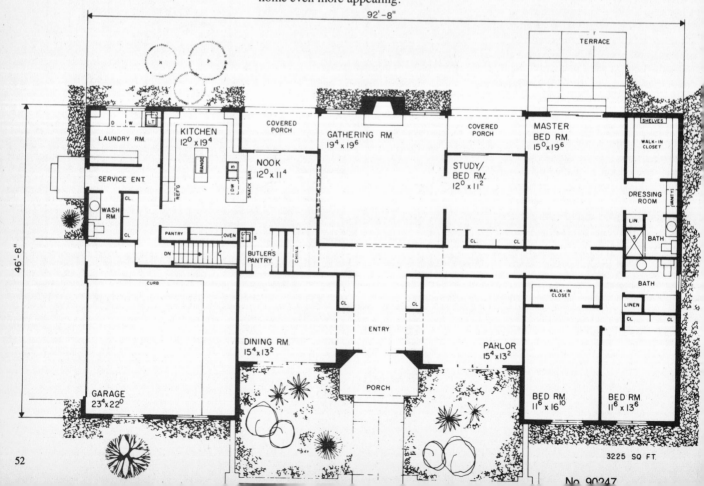

Spanish Home
Features Atrium

No. 90263

A centrally located interior atrium is one
of the most interesting features in this
Spanish design. The atrium has a built-in
seat and will bring light to the adjacent
rooms; living, dining, and breakfast.
Beyond the foyer, sunken one step, is a
tiled reception hall that includes a powder room. This area leads to the sleeping
wing and up one step to the family room.
Overlooking the family room is a railed
lounge, 279 square feet, which can be
used for various activities.

Main living area — 3,058 sq. ft.
Garage — 3 car

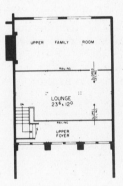

No. 90263

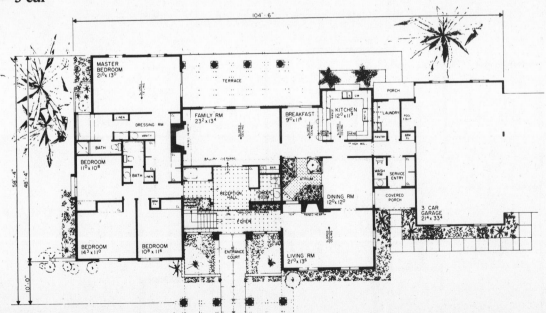

Inviting Porch Adorns Affordable Home

No. 90682

You don't have to give up storage space to build an affordable home. With large closets just inside the front door and in every bedroom, a walk-in pantry by the kitchen, and an extra-large storage area tucked behind the garage, you can build this house on an optional slab foundation and still keep the clutter to a minimum. The L-shaped living and dining room arrangement, brightened by triple windows and sliding glass doors, adds a spacious feeling to active areas. Eat in formal elegance overlooking the patio, or have a family meal in the country kitchen. Tucked in a private wing for a quiet bedtime atmosphere, three bedrooms and two full baths complete this affordable home loaded with amenities.

Living area — 1,160 sq. ft.
Garage — 2-car

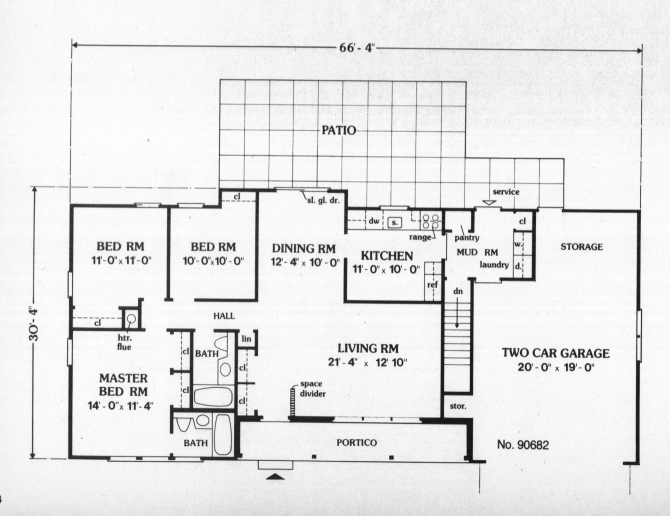

Zoned for Comfort

No. 90610

This ground-hugging ranch was designed for maximum use of the three basic living areas. The informal area —fireplaced family room, kitchen, and breakfast room— adjoins a covered porch. The fully-equipped kitchen is easily accessible to the formal dining room, which flows into the living room for convenient entertaining. Well-situated closets and bathrooms set the bedrooms apart from more active areas. The spacious master suite includes plenty of closet space and its own bath. The other bedrooms are served by the lavish hall bath equipped with two basins.

Main living area — 1,771 sq. ft.

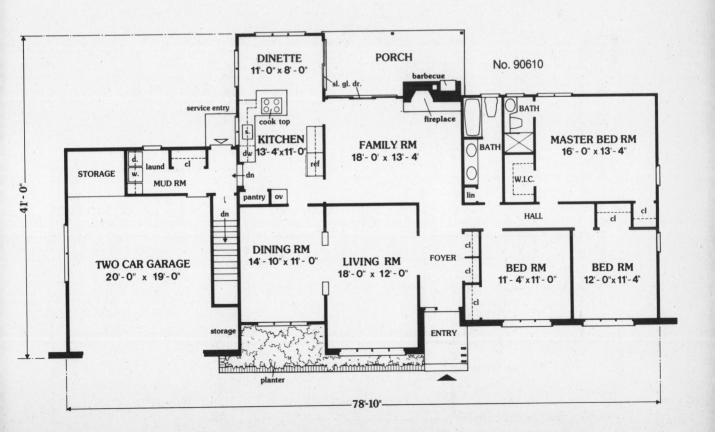

No. 90610

DINETTE 11'-0" x 8'-0"

PORCH

barbecue

fireplace

service entry

cook top

s.

BATH

KITCHEN 13'-4"x11'-0"

dw

FAMILY RM 18'-0' x 13'-4'

BATH

MASTER BED RM 16'-0" x 13'-4"

ref

STORAGE

d. w.

laund

cl

dn

W.I.C.

MUD RM

lin

pantry ov

dn

HALL

cl

cl

TWO CAR GARAGE 20'-0" x 19'-0"

DINING RM 14'-10" x 11'-0"

LIVING RM 18'-0" x 12'-0"

FOYER

cl

cl

BED RM 11'-4" x 11'-0"

BED RM 12'-0"x 11'-4"

cl

storage

ENTRY

41'-0"

planter

78'-10"

Cozy Traditional With Style

No. 99208

This charming one-story traditional home greets visitors with a covered porch. A galley-style kitchen shares a snack bar with the spacious gathering room where a fireplace is the focal point. An ample master suite includes a luxury bath with a whirlpool tub and separate dressing room. Two additional bedrooms, one that could double as a study, are located at the front of the home.

Basement — 1,830 sq. ft.
Garage — 2-car

Total living area — 1,830 sq. ft.

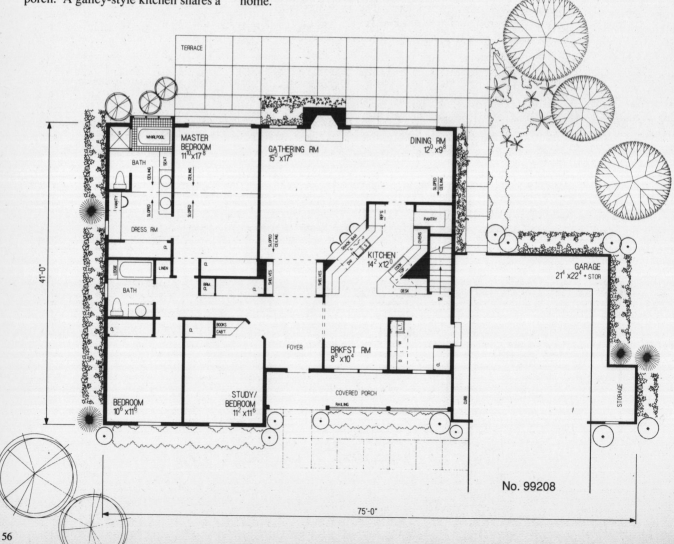

No. 99208

Classic Ranch with Convenience and Charm

No. 99224

This two or three bedroom home combines a care-free one floor lifestyle with those extra details that make entertaining for family and friends a pleasure. The extra-large gathering room is highlighted by a raised hearth fireplace, with extra hearth space for wood storage or warm-your-toes seating. The kitchen is surprisingly spacious, with a breakfast nook tucked in the sunny window bay. The backyard patio is reached via sliding doors from the master bedroom, living and dining rooms. A built-in vanity in the dressing area adds to the comfort of the master suite. And you'll find plenty of space for those special projects and hobbies in the storage/workshop alcove in the garage.

Basement — 2,006 sq. ft.
Garage — 546 sq. ft.
Plus storage

Total living area — 2,006 sq. ft.

No. 99224

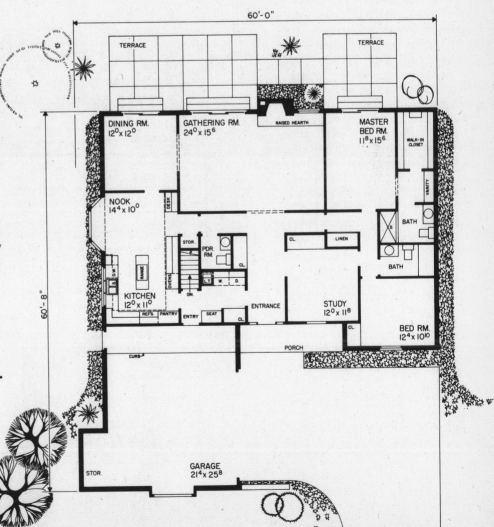

Retire to this Energy-Conscious Ranch

No. 99221

The air-lock entry hall, stone-floored greenhouse-sunspace, and plentiful skylights are just a few of the passive solar benefits of this 2-3 bedroom home. Orient the sunspace to face south on your site for optimum solar penetration; the stone floors will retain and radiate heat long into the night for winter comfort, while the extended eaves on the east side will provide good summer shading. You'll enjoy the open feeling of the skylit kitchen, with windows opening to the sunspace for lots of indirect lighting. The comfortable master bedroom offers a dressing area with sink, and a relaxing whirlpool in the bathroom. The third bedroom can be used as a study or library, and the two-car garage has a special area for additional storage or for use as a workshop.

Sun space — 216 sq. ft.
Basement — 1,632 sq. ft.
Garage — 2-car

Total living area — 1,632 sq. ft.

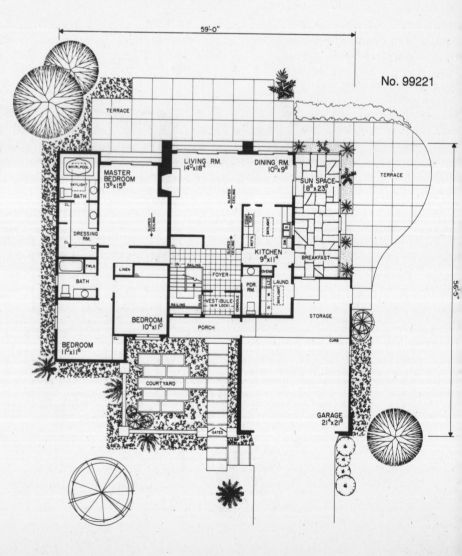

Enjoy the Space of a Two-Story Home on One Convenient Level

No. 99225

The impressive size of this three-to-four bedroom ranch encompasses a square-footage comparable to a two-story home. It's the right choice for a busy, growing family, with the option of turning the sitting room into a nursery or fourth bedroom. Take note of the fireplace linking the family and living rooms; the raised hearth extends well beyond the chimney on either side for a charming view-through to either room. The kitchen is a chef's delight; double wall ovens, walk-in pantry, snack bar, and center island sink and food preparation counter - all bathed in sunlight streaming through the three-window bay. The master suite combines a full bath and adjoining walk-in dressing closet for privacy and convenience, and features a private terrace reached through sliding glass doors. The tudor-style exterior detailing is carried through in the attached three-car garage. A cozy covered porch off the laundry room is a great spot for keeping an eye on the kids while you work.

Basement — 2,375 sq. ft.
Garage — 3-car

Total living area — 2,375 sq. ft.

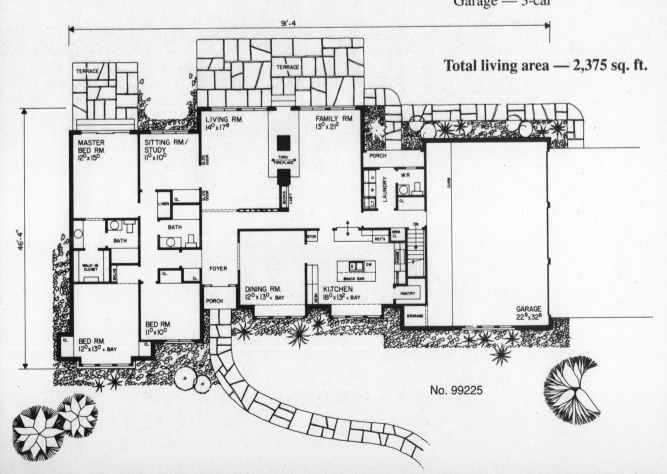

No. 99225

A Ranch Lover's Dream

No. 99244

There's a lot of room inside this traditional, three-bedroom ranch home. Families with small children will appreciate the connected family room and kitchen, with snack bar seating for four and easy monitoring of activities while making the evening meal. A formal dining room is the spot for guests and Sunday dinners. The first floor laundry off the family room is a great convenience - get household chores done while spending time with your family. Three ample bedrooms each fearure a walk-in closet, with a private full bath in the master suite. The living room is an inviting spot with a fireplace and row of windows looking out over the covered front porch. You'll find room for a small workshop in the garage alcove.

Basement — 1,949 sq. ft.
Garage — 2-car

Total living area — 1,949 sq. ft.

No. 99244

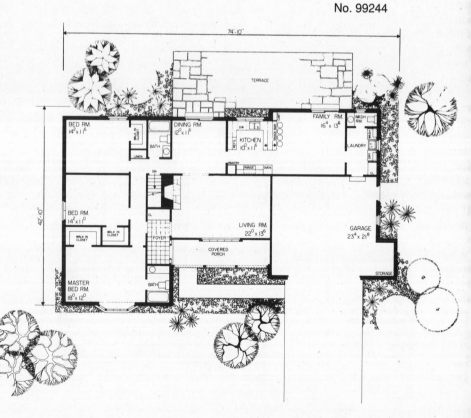

Unique Rooms Characterize this Ranch Home

No. 99246

This home design combines the best of ranch-style living with lots of luxurious space and special details for the family moving up. Consider the master suite: matching walk-in closets on either side of the dressing area, with a short walk to the whirlpool. Downstairs, the country kitchen will be the spot to gather, with ample seating space in front of the open fireplace, a four-seat breakfast bar, and cooking area that lets you stay with your guests while you whip up a gourmet feast. There's even a built-in alcove for the freezer. When dinner's done, gather around the living room hearth or retire to the custom media room with special cabinetry for all your audio and video equiptment. The "clutter" room will become one of your most treasured spots - it has room for laundry, workbench and tool storage, center work island, sewing area and lots of storage cupboards. And for the winter warmth and summer greenery, you'll enjoy the extra bonus of the greenhouse.

Greenhouse — 149 sq. ft.
Basement — 2,758 sq. ft.
Garage — 2-car

Total living area — 2,758 sq. ft.

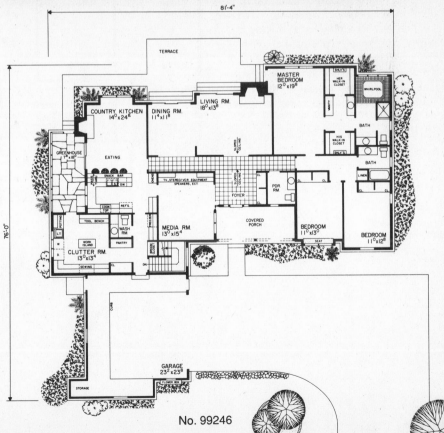

No. 99246

Easy one-floor living

No. 99216

A flexible floor plan and high-drama living areas characterize this two-to-three bedroom ranch. Behind the simple, arractive exterior is a surprisingly roomy home. Living areas are conveniently grouped in the right half of the house for everyday activities. The living room, with its vaulted ceiling and fireplace, opens to a spacious dining area to create a warm, comfortable family environment. The kitchen is designed for easy cooking, with a closet pantry, plenty of counter space and cupboards, and a pass-through to the adjacent breakfast room. The third bedroom, tucked off the entry foyer, could make a perfect home office of study.

Basement — 1,521 sq. ft.

Garage — 2-car

Total living area — 1,521 sq. ft.

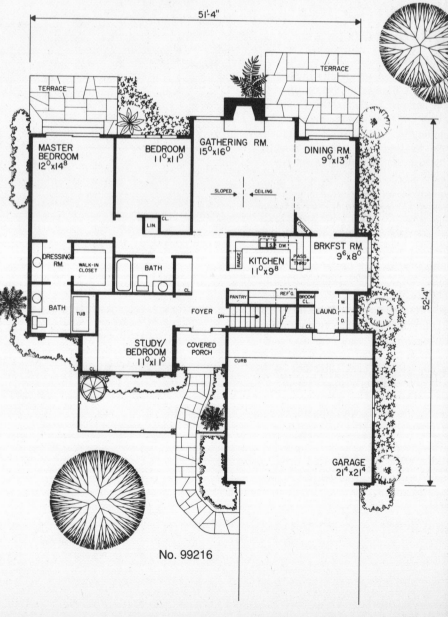

No. 99216

Great Layout, Great Family Home

No. 99227

A simple exterior masks an intriguing indoor setting in this surprisingly spacious three bedroom ranch. Enter beneath the curved porch into an open foyer with matched closets on either side. Directly ahead, a decorative wood screen sets off the big gathering room, reached via openings in the privacy screen. The large fireplace is flanked by sliding doors to the outdoor patio. Sleeping quarters are grouped in the right half of the house, with a master suite that offers lots of room for two, even on those hectic mornings. The rectilinear kitchen combines a breakfast nook and dining terrace, and a simple, yet highly efficient cooking area.

Basement — 1,746 sq. ft.

Garage — 2-car

Total living area — 1,746 sq. ft.

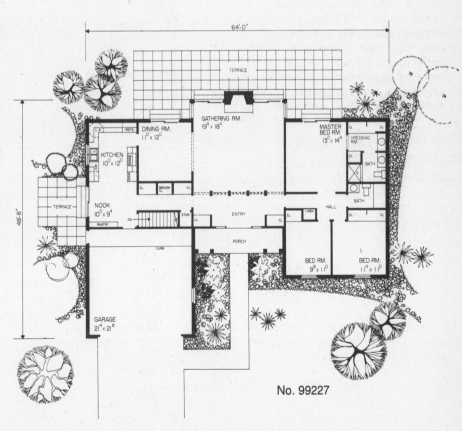

No. 99227

Striking Entryway

No. 20054

An expansive entrance with a cathedral ceiling in the living room offers a view of the entire house. The washer and dryer are located in the bedroom area, and even with small square footage, this home has a large master bedroom area and separating dining room and breakfast area. The deck is partially under the roof. The roof framing on this plan is simple, but the exterior is still interesting due to the large window and the farmhouse porch.

First floor — 1,461 sq. ft.
Basement — 1,435 sq. ft.
Garage — 528 sq. ft.

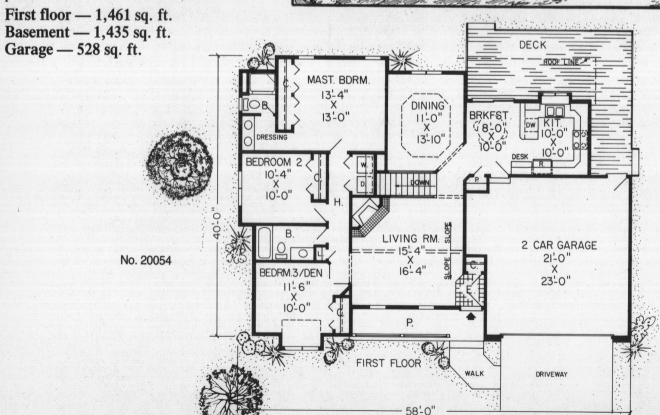

No. 20054

DECK
ROOF LINE

MAST. BDRM.
13'-4"
X
13'-0"

DRESSING

DINING
11'-0"
X
13'-10"

BRKFST.
8'-0"
X
10'-0"

KIT.
10'-0"
X
10'-0"

DESK

BEDROOM 2
10'-4"
X
10'-0"

W
D
DOWN

P.

BEDRM.3/DEN
11'-6"
X
10'-0"

LIVING RM.
15'-4"
X
16'-4"

SLOPE   SLOPE   SLOPE

2 CAR GARAGE
21'-0"
X
23'-0"

P.

40'-0"

FIRST FLOOR

WALK

DRIVEWAY

58'-0"

A Karl Kreeger Design

Compact Home
Has Open Design

No. 10455

The air lock entry saves energy and opens onto the tiled foyer which extends inward toward the adjacent dining and living rooms. The living room has a window wall which overlooks the lawn, a fireplace with hearth, built-in bookcases, a wetbar and direct access to the patio. The dining room has direct access to the step-saver kitchen with its plenti-ful storage and convenient peninsula. Along the opposite side of the house are the three bedrooms. Individual dressing areas within the master suite include separate vanities and walk-in closets.

First floor-1,643 sq. ft.
Garage-500 sq. ft.

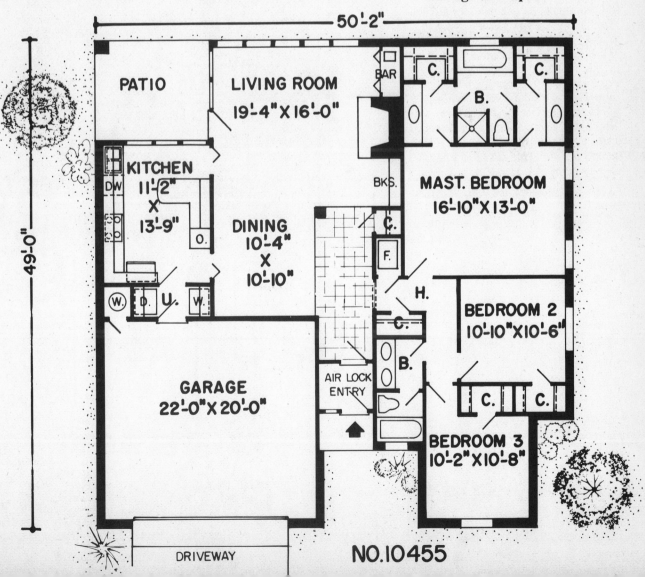

NO. 10455

Just the Right Size

No. 90524

You won't find any stairs in this gracious home for a retired couple, but you will find all the necessities you require. Two full bathrooms, for example, reward you with the privacy you've earned as well as make it easier to receive company. You'll find a spacious central entry, a fireplace for comfort and charm, an attached garage for security, a lovely patio directly off the dining room, and full laundry services just steps away. All these useful features are wrapped inside a distinctive home with the exterior stone work and Tudor windows of an English country home.

Living Area — 1,243 sq. ft.

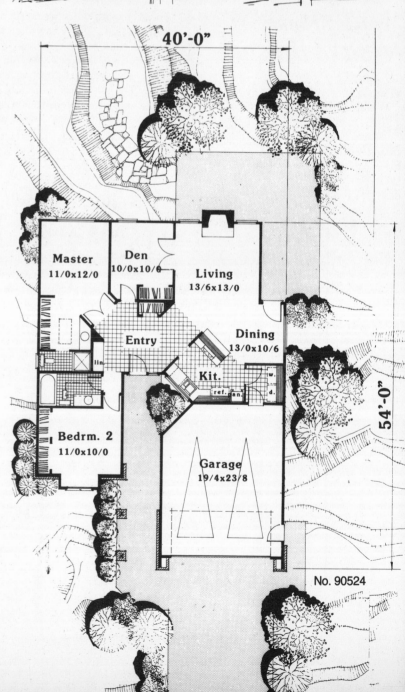

40'-0"

54'-0"

Master
11/0x12/0

Den
10/0x10/0

Living
13/6x13/0

Entry

Dining
13/0x10/6

Kit.

Bedrm. 2
11/0x10/0

Garage
19/4x23/8

No. 90524

Compact Step-Saver
Ideal for a Small Lot

No. 10775

From its easy-care exterior to its space-saving interior plan, this cozy gem is designed for convenience. Notice the step-saving laundry location, and the generous closet space and double vanities in the master suite. The central entry opens to a spacious kitchen-breakfast room combination with sliders to a walled garden. Beyond the kitchen, you'll find a formal dining room adjoining a fireplaced living room. Sliders lead to the rear patio, a perfect spot for warm-weather entertaining. Two bedrooms and two full baths are tucked behind the garage for a quiet atmosphere. You'll appreciate the private patio entrance off the master suite.

Main living area — 1,304 sq. ft.
Garage — one-car

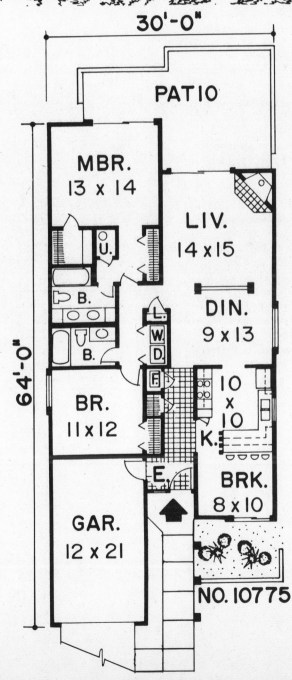

Daytime Delight

No. 91607

This exquisite, carefree home will be bathed in sunlight from dawn to dusk. The central foyer opens to a large, vaulted living and dining room arrangement that flows together for an open feeling accentuated by huge windows. French doors lend a quiet atmosphere to the front-facing den or bedroom off the foyer. You'll find two more bedrooms and two full baths just around the corner, past the utility room. Notice the exciting master suite with its vaulted ceiling and private double-vanitied bath. Informal areas overlooking the backyard include the soaring family room crowned by a fireplace, a glass-walled dining nook with access to a covered porch, and a kitchen that's centrally located for maximum convenience.

Main living area — 1,653 sq. ft.
Garage — 2-car

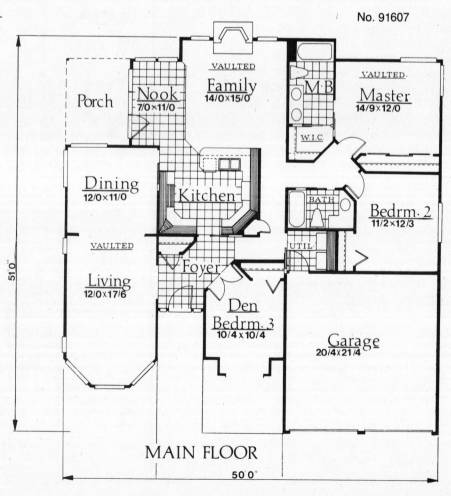

No. 91607

Porch

Nook
7/0 × 11/0

VAULTED
Family
14/0 × 15/0

M·B

W.I.C.

VAULTED
Master
14/9 × 12/0

Dining
12/0 × 11/0

Kitchen

BATH

Bedrm. 2
11/2 × 12/3

VAULTED
Living
12/0 × 17/6

Foyer

UTIL

Den
Bedrm. 3
10/4 × 10/4

Garage
20/4 × 21/4

51'0"

50'0"

MAIN FLOOR

Plant Shelf Divides Living Space with Greenery

No. 90394

Twin gables, a beautiful half-round window, and Colonial-style corner boards give this one-story classic an inviting, traditional exterior that says "Welcome." Inside, the ingenious, open plan of active areas makes every room seem even larger. Look at the vaulted living room, where floor-to-ceiling windows provide a pleasing unity with the yard. In the spectacular dining room, which adjoins the kitchen for convenient mealtimes, sliding glass doors open to a rear deck. Three bedrooms at the rear of the house include the angular master suite, which features a private bath and double-sized closet.

Basement — 1,252 sq. ft.
Garage — 2-car

Total living area — 1,252 sq. ft.

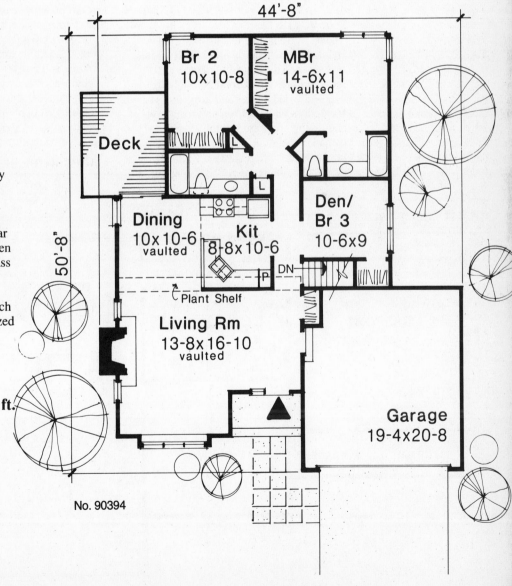

44'-8"

50'-8"

Br 2
10x10-8

MBr
14-6x11
vaulted

Deck

Dining
10x10-6
vaulted

Kit
8-8x10-6

Den/
Br 3
10-6x9

DN
P

Plant Shelf

Living Rm
13-8x16-10
vaulted

Garage
19-4x20-8

No. 90394

No Wasted Space

No. 90412

The open floor plan of this modified A-frame design virtually eliminated wasted hall space. The centrally located great room features a cathedral ceiling with exposed wood beams and large areas of fixed glass on both front and rear. Living and dining areas are virtually separated by a massive stone fireplace. The isolated master suite features a walk-in closet and sliding glass doors opening onto the front deck. A walk-thru utility room provides easy access from the carport and outside storage areas to the compact kitchen. On the opposite side of the great room are two additional bedrooms and a second full bath. A full-length deck and vertical wood siding with stone accents on the corners provide a rustic yet contemporary exterior. Specify crawlspace, basement or slab foundation when ordering.

Main living area — 1,454 sq. ft.

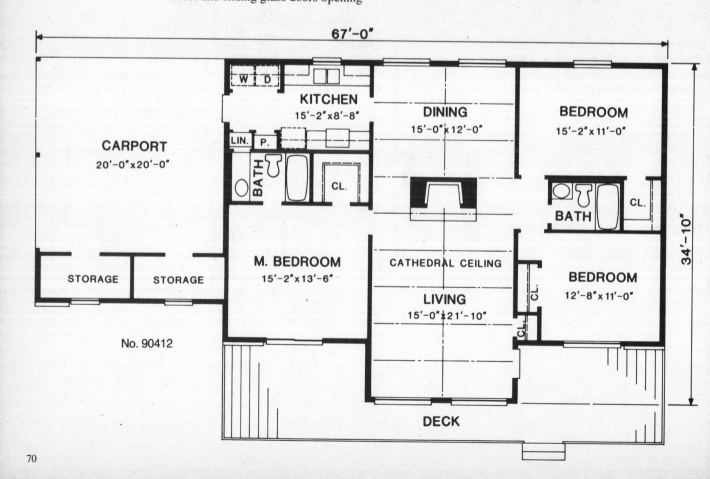

Compact Home is Surprisingly Spacious

No. 90905

Searching for a design where the living room takes advantage of both front and rear views? Look no further. And, this cozy ranch has loads of other features. An attractive porch welcomes guests and provides shade for the big living room window on hot summer days. A large covered sundeck adjacent to the living room, dining room and kitchen will make entertaining a delight. The roomy bedrooms, including the master suite with full bath and a walk-in closet, are protected from street noise by the two-car garage.

Main floor — 1,314 sq. ft.
Unfinished basement —
1,488 sq. ft.
Garage — 484 sq. ft.
Width — 50 ft.
Depth — 54 ft.

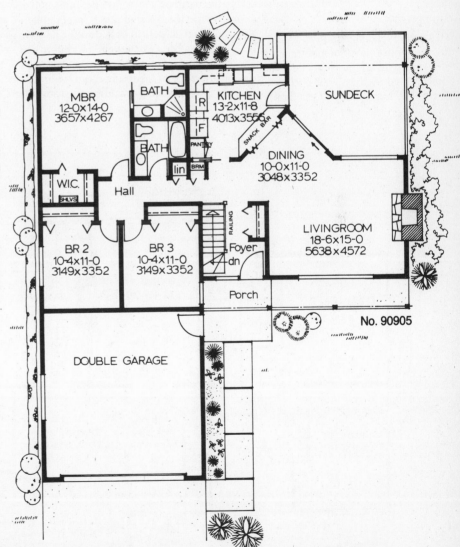

Easy Living, with a Hint of Drama

No. 90676

This one-level contemporary with a rustic, farmhouse flavor combines a touch of luxury with an informal plan. Watch the world go by from your kitchen vantage point, large enough for a family meal, and conveniently located for easy service to the formal dining room. When the weather's nice, use the built-in barbecue on the covered porch, accessible through sliders in both dining and living rooms. But, when there's a chill in the air, you'll enjoy the cozy, yet spacious ambience of the living room, with its exposed beams, crackling fire, and soaring, cathedral ceilings. You'll also appreciate the privacy of three bedrooms, down the hallway off the foyer. Hall and master baths feature convenient, split design and double-bowl vanities.

Living area — 1,575 sq. ft.
Garage — 2-car

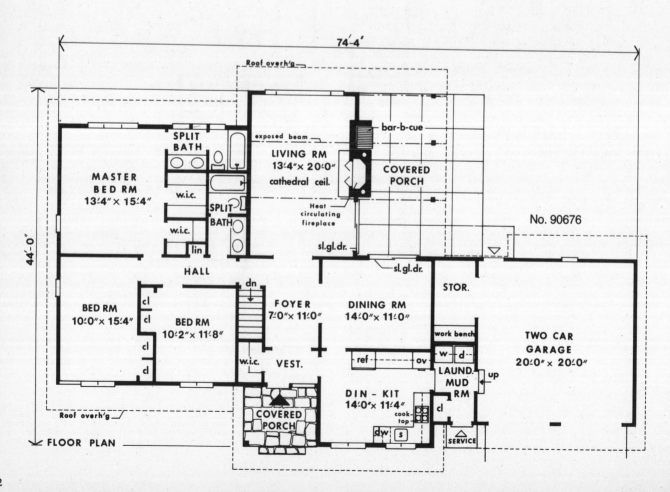

FLOOR PLAN

Zoned for Privacy

No. 20131

Here's a ranch home with a Tudor flavor. Active areas are centered off the foyer, with bedrooms tucked away in their own, private corners of the house. You'll find two bedrooms on a hallway off the foyer, each with walk-in closets, and just steps away from a full bath. The master suite, located behind the garage for a quiet atmosphere, features a bath with step-in shower, garden tub, and double vanities. The front-facing living room boasts high ceilings and a cozy fireplace. The dining room adjoins the kitchen and breakfast bay for mealtime convenience. Notice the built-in china cabinet, the elegant ceiling treatments in the dining and living rooms, and the rear deck that's a perfect place for a barbecue.

Basement — 1,837 sq. ft.
Garage — 477 sq. ft.

Total living area —1,862 sq. ft.

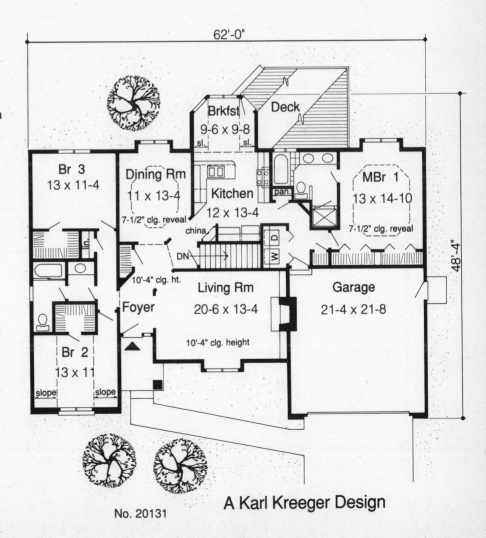

62'-0"

48'-4"

Br 3
13 x 11-4

Dining Rm
11 x 13-4
7-1/2" clg. reveal

Brkfst
9-6 x 9-8
sl.   sl.

Deck

Kitchen
12 x 13-4

pan.

MBr 1
13 x 14-10
7-1/2" clg. reveal

china

DN

10'-4" clg. ht.

W D

Foyer

Living Rm
20-6 x 13-4
10'-4" clg. height

Garage
21-4 x 21-8

Br 2
13 x 11
slope   slope

No. 20131

A Karl Kreeger Design

Ideal for Formal Entertaining

No. 90421

This lovely French Provincal design features a formal foyer flanked by the living room on one side and the dining room on the other. A family room with a raised-hearth fireplace and double doors to the patio, and the L-shaped island kitchen with breakfast bay and open counter to the family room allow for more casual living. Adjacent to the breakfast bay is a utility room with outside entrance. The master suite includes one double closet and a compartmentalized bath with a walk-in closet, step-up garden tub, double vanity and linen closet. Two front bedrooms and a second full bath with a linen closet complete the design. A recessed entry and circular porch add to the formal exterior.

Area — 1,940 sq. ft.

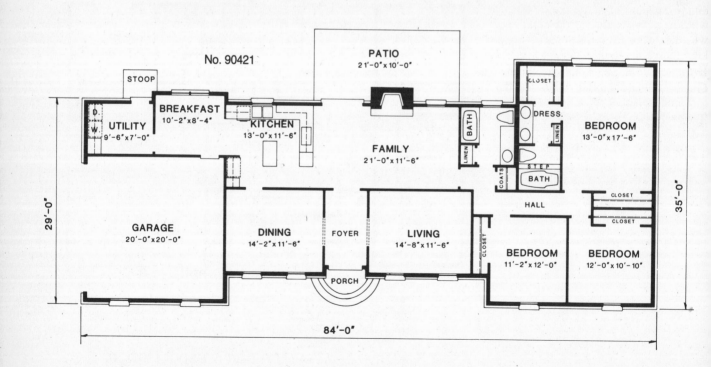

Easy-Care Elegance

No. 20127

Brick and clapboard siding give this one-level beauty a sturdy, traditional flair. Step from the sheltered porch to a central foyer. To the right, you'll find two bedrooms and a full, double-vanitied bath. Walk straight into the living room, which features a wetbar, a fireplace, and distinctive, high ceilings. Overlooking the backyard, the master suite boasts special ceiling treatments, a room-size walk-in closet, and a full bath loaded with amenities. A formal dining room and breakfast nook, each with decorative ceilings and bump-out windows, conveniently flank the kitchen with adjoining deck.

Basement — 1,917 sq. ft.

Garage — 484 sq. ft.

Total living area — 1,934 sq. ft.

No. 20127

58'-0"

55'-10"

Deck

5-1/2" clg. reveal

Kit 11-10 x 12-8

pan.

Dining 12 x 11-4

MBr 1 13 x 15-4

7-1/2" clg. reveal

Living Rm 10'-4" clg. ht. 23-6 x 13-8

desk

Brkfst 11-4 x 9 1-1/2" clg. reveal

W D

L

DN

bar lin.

Foyer

Garage 21-4 x 21-8

Br 3 / Den 11-4 x 12 sl sl

Br 2 11-6 x 12-10

First Floor

A Karl Kreeger Design

Inexpensive Ranch Design

No. 20062

This attractive, inexpensive ranch home has a brick and vertical siding exterior. The interior has a well set-up kitchen area with its own breakfast area by a large picture window. A formal dining room is located near the kitchen. The living room has one open beam across a sloping ceiling. A large hearth is in front of a woodburning fireplace. Inside the front entrance a tiled foyer incorporates closet space and has many different room entrances through which an individual can walk. The master bedroom has an extremely large bath area with its own walk-in closet. Two other bedrooms share a full bath. There is also a linen closet and a closet for the washer and dryer area. A two-car garage is offered in this plan.

First floor — 1,500 sq. ft.
Basement — 1,500 sq. ft.
Garage — 482 sq. ft.

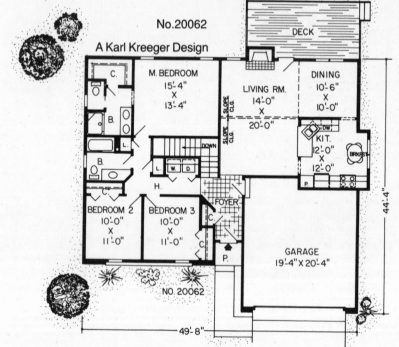

No. 20062

A Karl Kreeger Design

Deck Doubles
Outdoor Living Space

No. 10619

This one-level contemporary is a one-of-a-kind design just made for the sun lover. With a huge front deck featuring pass-through convenience from the kitchen, a rear patio, and an abundance of windows, you're guaranteed a cheerful atmosphere, even on the coldest day. The central focus of this contemporary charmer is the sunken living room, with its three window walls and massive fireplace. Open to the kitchen, foyer, and handy bar area, this elegant room seems even larger because of its soaring ceiling. And, just behind the fireplace, an indoor hot tub turns the skylit sunspace into a private spa. The foyer separates active areas from the front bedroom and vaulted master suite. Another bedroom shares a quiet spot behind the garage with a full bath and utility area.

First floor — 2,352 sq. ft.
Basement — 2,352 sq. ft.
Garage — 696 sq. ft.

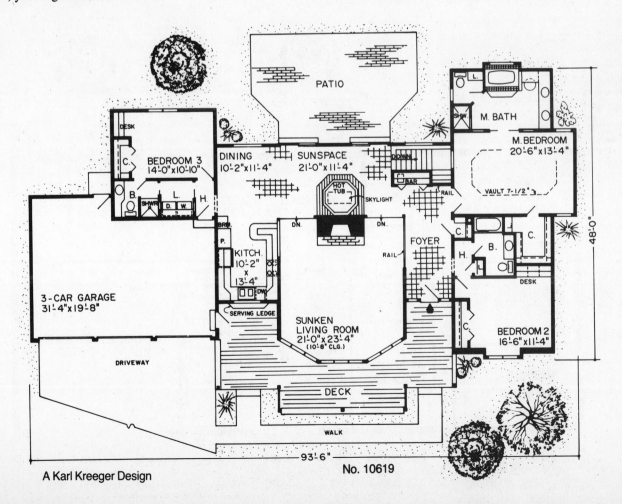

A Karl Kreeger Design   No. 10619

Family Room Forms Core

No. 1064

The family room forms the core of this plan. Creating the focal point in this room is a heat circulating fireplace, encased in masonry and faced with cut stone. Bookshelves, a TV shelf and wood storage area fit into the stone flanking the fireplace. The family room flows through an eating bar to the kitchen. A utility room is handily tucked around the corner behind the kitchen. Secluded on the other side of the family room are three bedrooms, a bath and a master suite.

First floor — 1,954 sq. ft.
Garage — 431 sq. ft.

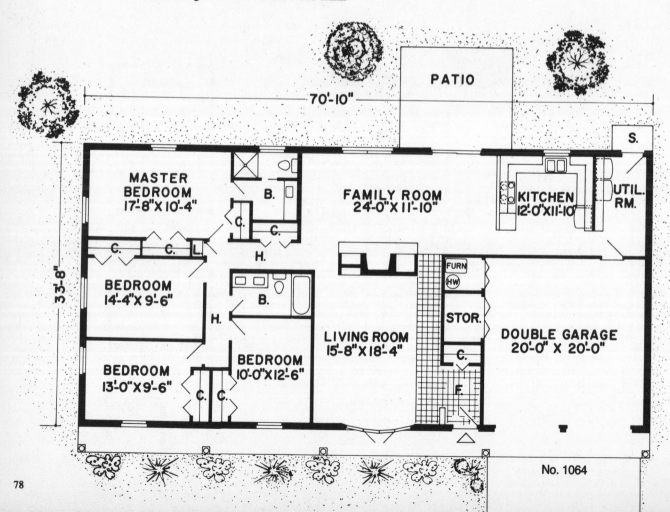

No. 1064

Soaring Ceilings Add Space and Drama

No. 90288

Here's a one-level home with an airy feeling accentuated by oversized windows and well-placed skylights. You'll love the attractive garden court that adds privacy to the front facing bedroom, the sheltered porch that opens to a central foyer, and the wide-open active areas. Two bedrooms, tucked down a hall off the foyer, include the sunny master suite with its sloping ceilings, private terrace entry, and luxurious garden bath with adjoining dressing room. The gathering room, study, and formal dining room flow together along the rear of the house, sharing the warmth of the gathering room fireplace, and a magnificent view of the terrace. Convenient pass-throughs add to the efficiency of the galley kitchen and adjoining breakfast room.

Living area — 1,387 sq. ft.
Garage — 2-car

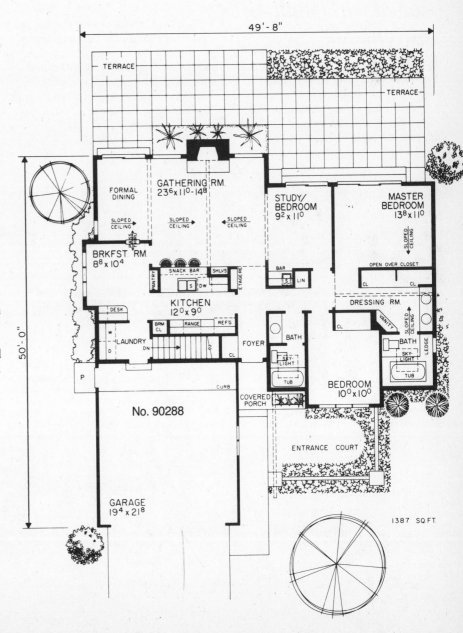

Loaded with Built-In Convenience

No. 90242

This brick ranch touched with Tudor accents boasts a bright, sunny atmosphere and insures your privacy, too. Bedrooms share a separate wing off the entry with two full baths. Notice the private terrace off the master suite, a plus you're sure to appreciate. Living and dining rooms span the front of the house in an open plan separated only by built-in shelves. Both enjoy the warmth of the two-way fireplace that also opens to the rear-facing family room. Look at the well-appointed kitchen, situated between the nook and family room, and just steps away from the dining room. Walking past the service entrance, laundry, and powder room, you'll find a room with possibilities that will spur your imagination.

Living area — 2,747 sq. ft.
Garage — 2-car

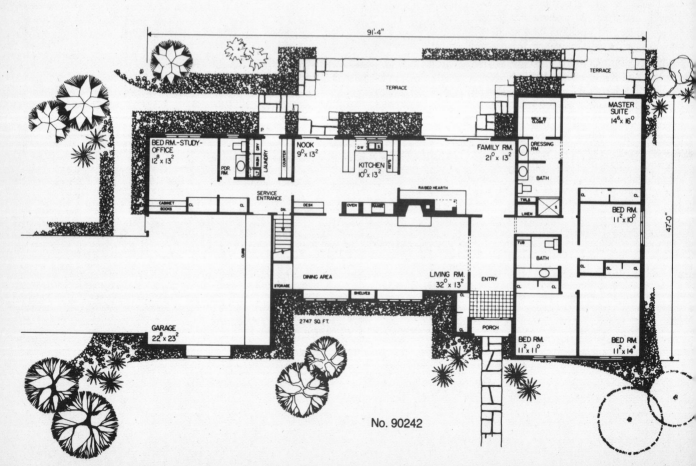

No. 90242

Rustic Flavor Inside and Out

No. 90212

There's plenty of room for family and friends in this handsome, one-level home. Entertain in the elegant atmosphere of the fireplaced, sunken living room off the entry. Show your guests into the adjoining formal dining room one step up. You'll enjoy endless family hours in the rustic, informal area at the rear of the house, which includes a comfortable family room, an efficient kitchen-breakfast room combination, and fieldstone terrace. In a quiet wing off the entry, you'll find four bedrooms and two full baths with double vanities. You'll appreciate your own private terrace off the master suite. Notice all the added storage throughout this home.

Living area — 2,282 sq. ft.
Garage — 2-car

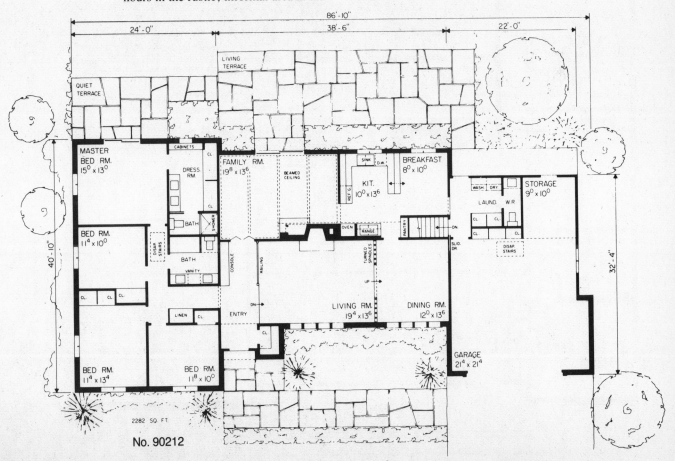

No. 90212

L-Shaped Bungalow With Two Porches

No. 90407

Pleasing L-shaped design indicates a smooth flowing floor plan. Master suite includes garden tub, shower, his and her vanities and separate walk-in closets. Two other bedrooms and a full bath complete the sleeping wing. A large family room, separate foyer, living and dining combine to form the center section. U-shaped kitchen, breakfast nook with bay window and separate utility complete the plan. Specify basement, crawlspace or slab foundation when ordering.

Area — 1,950 sq. ft.

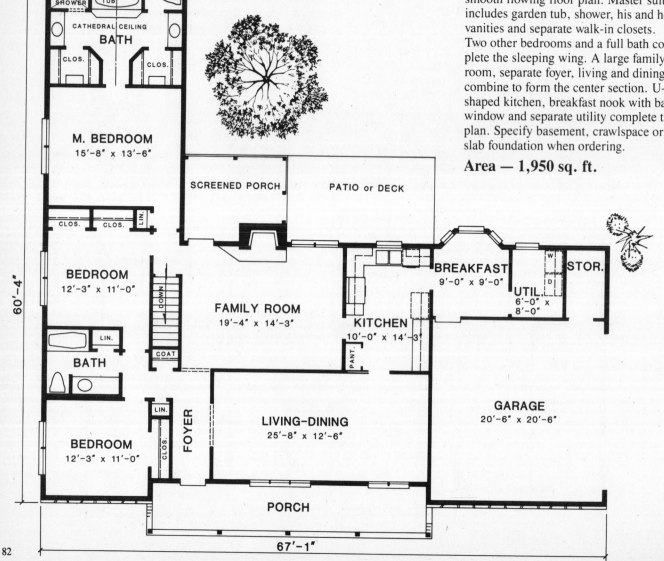

SHOWER   GARDEN TUB

CATHEDRAL CEILING
BATH

CLOS.   CLOS.

M. BEDROOM
15'-8" x 13'-6"

SCREENED PORCH   PATIO or DECK

CLOS.   CLOS.   LIN.

BEDROOM
12'-3" x 11'-0"

DOWN

LIN.

BATH

COAT

BEDROOM
12'-3" x 11'-0"

60'-4"

FAMILY ROOM
19'-4" x 14'-3"

KITCHEN
10'-0" x 14'-3"

PANT.

BREAKFAST
9'-0" x 9'-0"

UTIL.
6'-0" x 8'-0"

W   STOR.
D

LIN.

CLOS.

FOYER

LIVING-DINING
25'-8" x 12'-6"

GARAGE
20'-6" x 20'-6"

PORCH

67'-1"

Angular Excitement

No. 20307

It's easy to find the entry to this attractive clapboard home. It's nestled in an alcove between the dining room and bedroom. Step inside the vaulted vestibule to the skylit atrium, the dazzling focal point of this cheerful home. To the left, you'll find an enormous kitchen that serves both the formal dining room and breakfast room with ease. A covered porch and adjoining deck add lots of outdoor living space, perfect for barbecues or warm-weather gatherings. When there's a chill in the air, entertain in the spacious, vaulted living room, warmed by the glow of a huge fireplace. Reach the bedroom wing, characterized by generous windows, ample closet space, and two full baths, from a hallway off the atrium.

Basement — 1,567 sq. ft.

Garage — 500 sq. ft.

Total living area — 1,680 sq. ft.

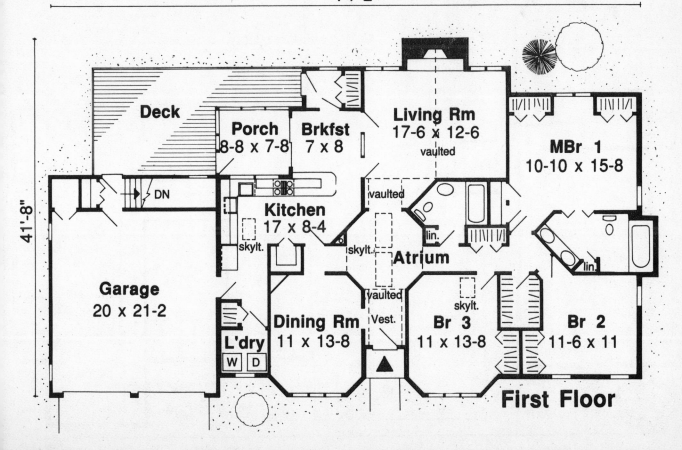

Covered Drive And Entrance Add Touch Of Elegance To Spanish Ranch

No. 10536

An impressive covered entry leading to the tiled foyer highlights the luxury of this four-bedroom home. Two patios offer ample space for outdoor entertaining. Adjacent to a roomy kitchen with the convenience of an island and plenty of cabinet space, is the hearth room which doubles as an informal dining area and family room. Additional family living spaces are incorporated into the large great room and the formal dining room with its built-in hutch and corner china cabinet. Each of the four bedrooms has a private bath. A scenic garden court divides bedrooms three and four.

First floor—3,972 sq. ft.
Basement—3,972 sq. ft.
Garage—924 sq. ft.

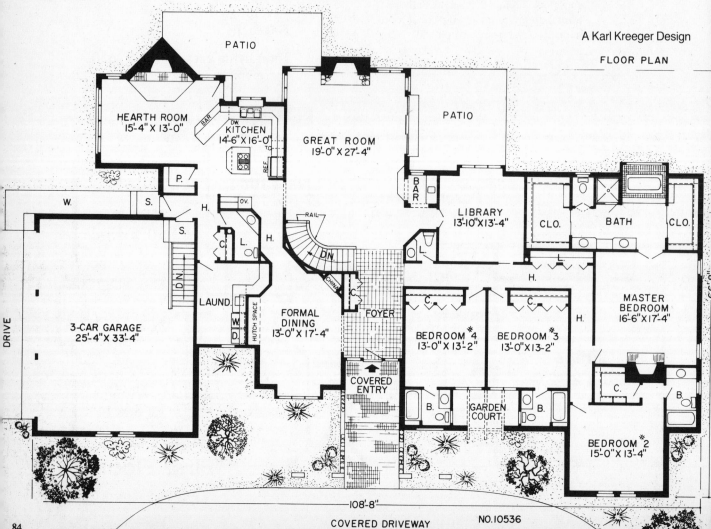

A Karl Kreeger Design

FLOOR PLAN

Build Now, Plan for Tomorrow

No. 10612

Here's a rambling country farmhouse that will house your family in casual comfort, and allow for future expansion. The staircase dominating the central foyer not only leads to an 1,100 square foot attic, it provides a noise buffer for the three bedrooms down the hall to the left. Designed to accommodate a crowd, this plan allows easy access to every room from the foyer. Formal living and dining rooms at the front of the house are nice for entertaining, but the massive family room with its twin sliders to the outdoor patio is a cozy spot to gather around a crackling fire. Enjoy family suppers in the sunny nook adjoining the kitchen, which serves both dining rooms with ease.

Basement — 2,730 sq. ft.
Garage — 653 sq. ft.

Total living area — 2,730 sq. ft.

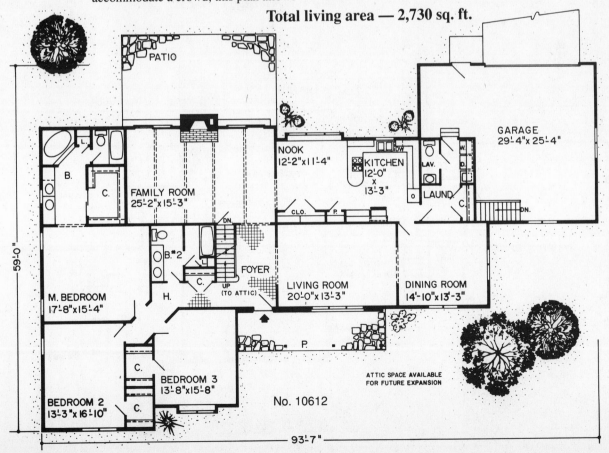

PATIO

NOOK 12'-2"x11'-4"

KITCHEN 12'-0" x 13'-3"

GARAGE 29'-4"x 25'-4"

LAV.

LAUND.

B.

C.

FAMILY ROOM 25'-2"x15'-3"

CLO.

P.

DN.

B.#2

C.

FOYER

UP (TO ATTIC)

LIVING ROOM 20'-0"x 13'-3"

DINING ROOM 14'-10"x13'-3"

M. BEDROOM 17'-8"x15'-4"

H.

59'-0"

C.

BEDROOM 3 13'-8"x15'-8"

P.

ATTIC SPACE AVAILABLE FOR FUTURE EXPANSION

No. 10612

BEDROOM 2 13'-3"x 16'-10"

C.

93'-7"

Window Boxes Add Romantic Charm

No. 90684

Practical yet pretty, this ranch home separates active and quiet areas for privacy when you want it. To the left, off the central foyer, you'll find a formal living and dining room combination that's just perfect for entertaining. The wing to the right of the foyer includes three spacious bedrooms and two full baths. Sunlight and warmth pervade the open, informal areas at the rear of the house, where the kitchen, dining bay, and family room enjoy the benefits of a large fireplace and an expansive glass wall overlooking the patio. When the kids come home after a day's play, you'll appreciate the convenient lavatory location just inside the back door. There's plenty of storage space in the garage, just past the mud-room off the kitchen.

Living area — 1,486 sq. ft.
Garage — 2-car

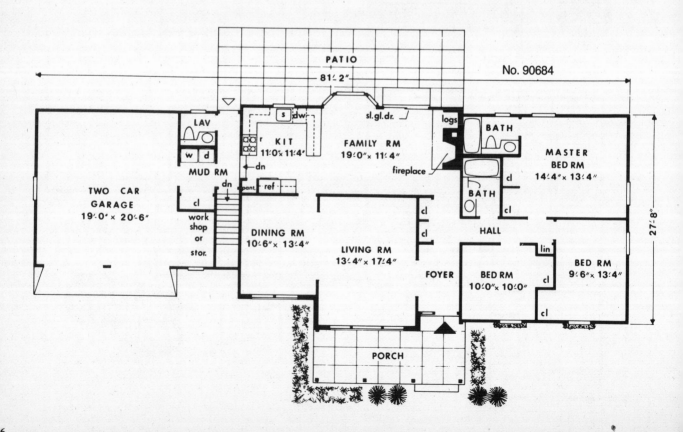

Bring the Outdoors In

No. 20177

Even though this natural beauty offers easy-care living on one level, its high ceilings and stacked windows make it feel like a two-story home. The skylit, central foyer, tucked between the three-car garage and bedroom wing, leads straight into a magnificent living room that accommodates every activity. Bookshelves and a TV cabinet share one wall with a fireplace; there's a wetbar that saves steps when you're entertaining; and easy access to the adjoining wood deck is a plus you'll appreciate when the weather's nice. The kitchen, with its built-in ovens, pantry, and cooktop island, is a gourmet's dream. And privacy is assured with the separate wing that houses the three bedrooms and two full baths.

Basement — 2,457 sq. ft.
Garage — 846 sq. ft.

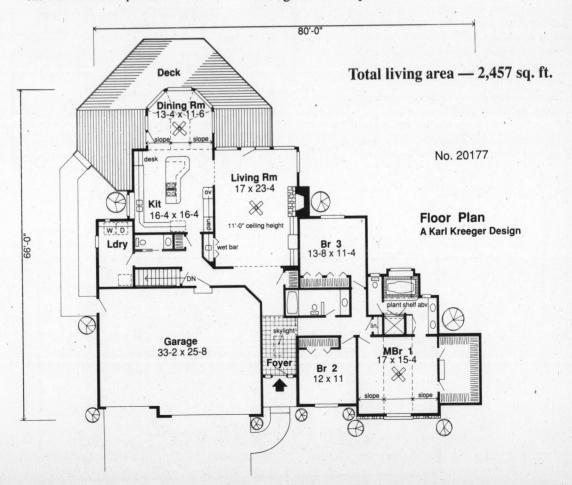

Total living area — 2,457 sq. ft.

No. 20177

Floor Plan
A Karl Kreeger Design

Outdoor-Lovers' Delight

No. 10748

This one-level charmer packs a lot of convenience into a compact space. From the shelter of the front porch, the foyer leads three ways: right to the bedroom wing, left to the roomy kitchen and dining room, or straight ahead to the massive living room. You'll appreciate the quiet atmosphere in the sleeping wing, the elegant recessed ceilings and private bath in the master suite, and the laundry facilities that adjoin the bedrooms. You'll enjoy the convenience of a kitchen with a built-in pantry and adjacent dining room. And, you'll love the airy atmosphere in the sunny, fireplaced living room, which features a cooling fan, high ceilings, and double French doors to the huge, wrap-around porch.

Main living area — 1,540 sq. ft.
Porches — 530 sq. ft.

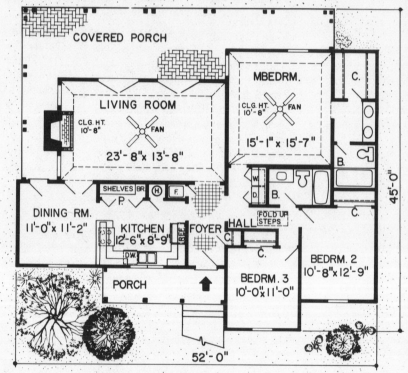

COVERED PORCH

LIVING ROOM
CLG. HT. 10'-8"
FAN
23'-8" x 13'-8"

MBEDRM.
CLG. HT. 10'-8"
FAN
15'-1" x 15'-7"

C.

B.

SHELVES
BR
H
F.
P.

W.
D.
B.

DINING RM.
11'-0" x 11'-2"

KITCHEN
12'-6" x 8'-9"
D.W.
REF.

FOYER

HALL
FOLD UP STEPS
C.

C.

BEDRM. 2
10'-8" x 12'-9"

PORCH

BEDRM. 3
10'-0" x 11'-0"

45'-0"

52'-0"

No. 10748

88

Roomy Ranch Design

No. 10594

This delightful ranch design utilizes space with great efficiency. Enter a tiled foyer and be greeted by an excellent floor plan designed to handle traffic. Off the foyer to the right, the great room has a sloping open beamed ceiling and a wood burning fireplace. A den/bedroom lies to the left of the foyer. Connected to the great room is the dining room and the kitchen. Sliding glass doors lead from the dining room out onto a large wooden deck. Other features in this plan include a laundry room and two other bedrooms that have their own full baths. A two-car garage is also added for convenience.

First — 1,565 sq. ft.
Basement — 1,576 sq. ft.
Garage — 430 sq. ft.

A Karl Kreeger Design

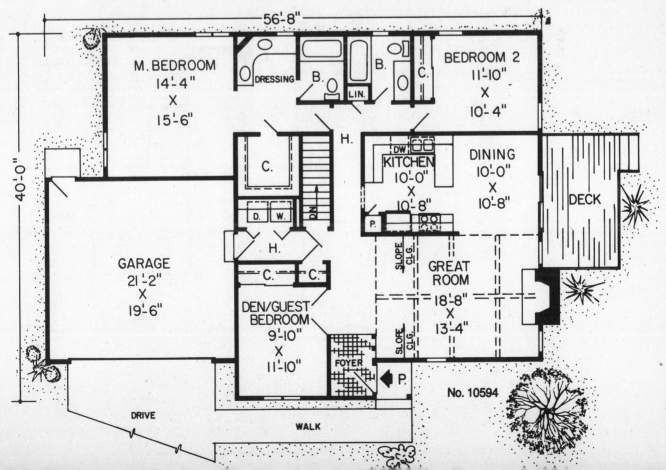

Varied Roof Heights Create Interesting Lines

No. 90601

This rambling one-story Colonial farmhouse packs a lot of living space into its compact plan. The covered porch, enriched by arches, columns and Colonial details, is the focal point of the facade. Inside, the house is zoned for convenience. Formal living and dining rooms occupy the front of the house. To the rear are the family room, island kitchen, and dinette. The family room features a heat-circulating fireplace, visible from the entrance foyer, and sliding glass doors to the large rear patio. Three bedrooms and two baths are away from the action in a private wing.

Total living area — 1,536 sq. ft (Optional slab construction available)

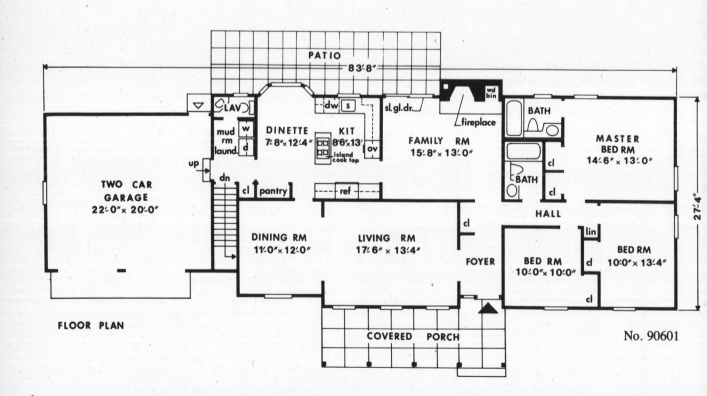

FLOOR PLAN

No. 90601

Classic and Convenient

No. 20110

Who said one-level homes had to be boring rectangles? Here's a clapboard and brick beauty with loads of curbside appeal. Step inside to a spacious living room dominated by a corner fireplace. A hallway off the foyer leads to two bedrooms, a full bath, and lots of closet space. At the rear of the house, you'll find a formal dining room and skylit breakfast nook adjoining the kitchen, a step-saving convenience for busy cooks. The rear deck is a nice spot for a barbeque, or just plain relaxing. And, when you really need an escape at the end of a hectic day, retire to your private master suite, complete with a double vanitied bath, a raised tub, and a walk-in shower.

First floor — 1,786 sq. ft.
Basement — 1,786 sq. ft.
Garage — 484 sq. ft.

No. 20110

A Karl Kreeger Design

DECK

BRK.
9'-0" x 8'-6"

SKYLIGHTS

KITCHEN
17'-0" x 9'-0"

DINING
10'-0" x 12'-4"

7-1/2" CLG. REV.

7-1/2" CLG. REVEAL

B.

MBR.
16'-0" x 12'-8"

W. D.

BR. 3
11'-4"x11'-6"

HALL

B.

LIVING ROOM
20'-0" x 14'-4"

GARAGE
21'-8" x 21'-8"

FOYER

LEDGE

BR. 2
11'-4"x12'-0"

SLOPE   LEVEL   SLOPE

49'-0"

62'-0"

Flexible Plan Create Many Options

No. 90324

Add a third bedroom, include a cozy den, or expand the dining area according to the family's needs. This flexible plan is designed to let you decide. The inviting great room views blooming plants in season through the multiple windows and features a vaulted ceiling plus a fireplace and built-in bookcase. The roomy eat-in kitchen opens onto the partially enclosed deck through sliding glass doors. Its L-shaped design provides for convenient meal preparation and easy access to storage. The comfortable master bedroom has a private bath, large walk-in closet and charming window seat. The second full bath is convenient to the second bedroom as well as the living areas of the house.

Living area — 1,016 sq. ft.

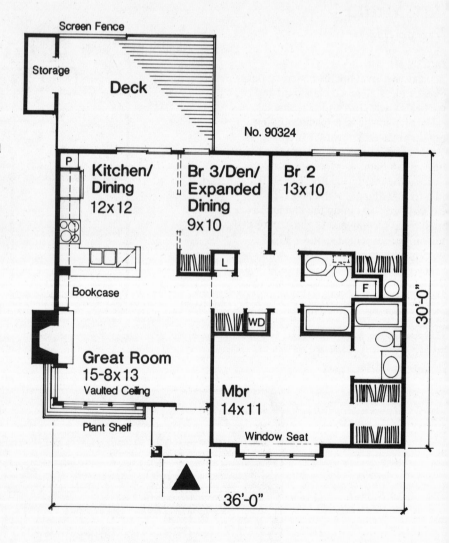

Screen Fence

Storage

Deck

No. 90324

Kitchen/Dining 12x12

Br 3/Den/Expanded Dining 9x10

Br 2 13x10

Bookcase

Great Room 15-8x13 Vaulted Ceiling

Mbr 14x11

Plant Shelf

Window Seat

30'-0"

36'-0"

Amenities Galore

No. 20120

Can't you imagine enjoying the sunny atmosphere in the dining room of this handsome, one-level gem? Vaulted ceilings, windows on three sides, and a convenient open arrangement with the kitchen make this a special room with an outdoor feeling, in a house with loads of character. And, the adjoining deck adds outdoor living space when the weather's nice. A wood-burning fireplace is the focus of the adjoining living room, and provides a little extra help with the heating bills. Three bedrooms and two full baths lie at the rear of the house, away from the activity of the street. Notice the extra amenities in the master bath: double vanities, a step-in shower, and a garden tub.

Basement — 1,356 sq. ft.
Garage — 507 sq. ft.

Total living area — 1,363 sq. ft.

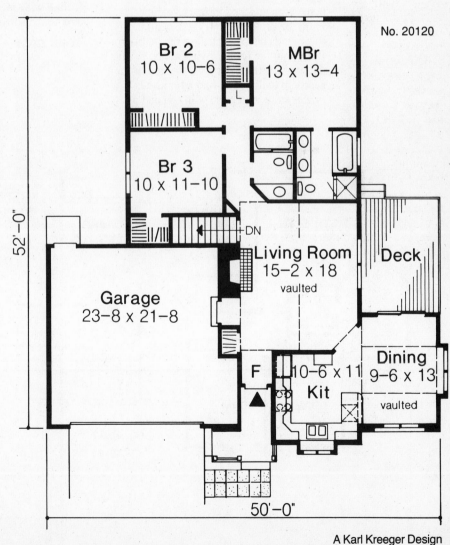

No. 20120

Br 2
10 x 10–6

MBr
13 x 13–4

Br 3
10 x 11–10

DN

Living Room
15–2 x 18
vaulted

Deck

Garage
23–8 x 21–8

F

10–6 x 11
Kit

Dining
9–6 x 13
vaulted

52'–0"

50'–0"

A Karl Kreeger Design

Indoor/Outdoor Unity

No. 91011

One-level living has never been more interesting than in this three-bedroom home with attached three-car garage. From the protected entry, the central foyer leads down the hall to the bedroom wing, into the formal living areas, or into the sun-washed library. At the end of the bedroom hall, you'll find a luxurious master suite, complete with spa and a private deck. Straight ahead, glass walls and an open plan unite the formal dining and sunken living rooms with the back yard. The adjoining island kitchen, nook, and family room continue the outdoor feeling with expansive windows and sliders to the surrounding covered patio.

Total area — 2,242 sq. ft.

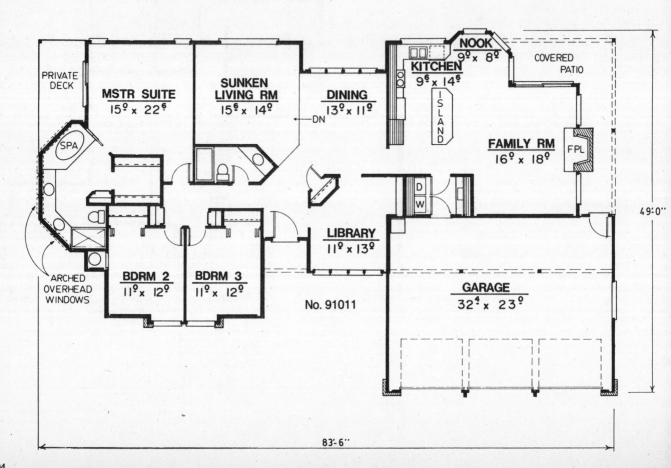

One-Level Convenience

No. 91025

This cheerful sun-catcher is sure to please your family. Oversized windows flood every room with warmth and light. Bay windows and angled walls create interesting shapes in the family living areas that surround the central entry. At mealtime, you'll appreciate the kitchen, tucked between the formal dining room and breakfast nook for maximum efficiency. And, when bedtime rolls around, you'll enjoy the separation of active and quiet areas. Double doors, double sinks, and a room-sized walk-in closet make the master suite an attractive retreat for the masters of the house. This plan is built on a crawlspace foundation.

Garage — 2-car

Total living area — 1,782 sq. ft.

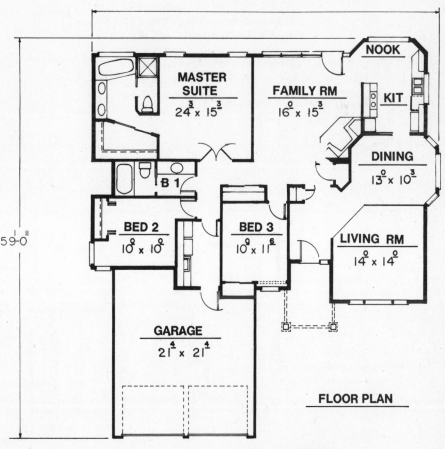

FLOOR PLAN

No. 91025

Your Classic Hideaway

No. 90423

Don't limit this design. Such a tranquil plan could maximize a vacation or suit retirement, as well as be a wonderful family home. It's large enough to welcome a crowd, but small enough for easy upkeep. The only stairs go to the basement. The lavish master suite, with its sunken tub, melts away cares. Either guest bedroom is big enough for two. The lovely fireplace is both cozy and a source of heat for the core area of the home. Note how the country kitchen connects to the large dining and living space. With a screened porch, laundry alcove, and large garage for storage, you'll have everything you need with a minimum of maintenance and cleaning. Specify basement, crawlspace, or slab foundation.

Living area — 1,773 sq. ft.
Screened porch — 240 sq. ft.

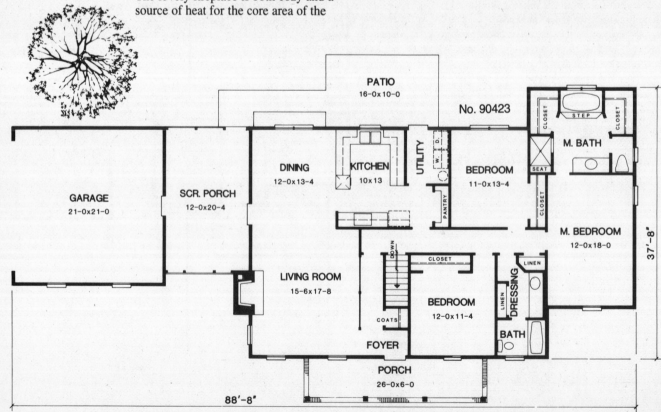

Carefree Comfort

No. 91418

Easy living awaits you in this one-level traditional designed with privacy in mind. A dramatic, vaulted foyer separates active areas from the three bedrooms. Down the skylit hall lies the master suite, where you'll discover the luxury of a private patio off the book-lined reading nook, decorative ceilings, and a well-appointed bath. The soaring roof line of the foyer continues into the great room, which combines with the bayed dining room to create a celebration of open space enhanced by abundant windows. The cook in the house will love the rangetop island kitchen and nook arrangement, loaded with storage inside, and surrounded by a built-in planter outside that's perfect for an herb garden.

**Main living area — 1,665 sq. ft.
Garage — 1-car**

ALTERNATE BASEMENT PLAN

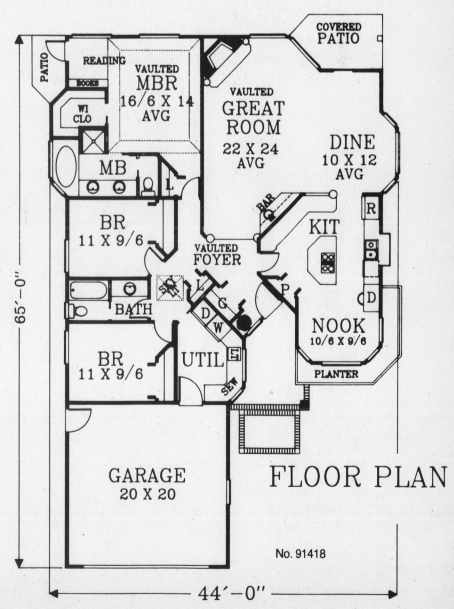

FLOOR PLAN

No. 91418

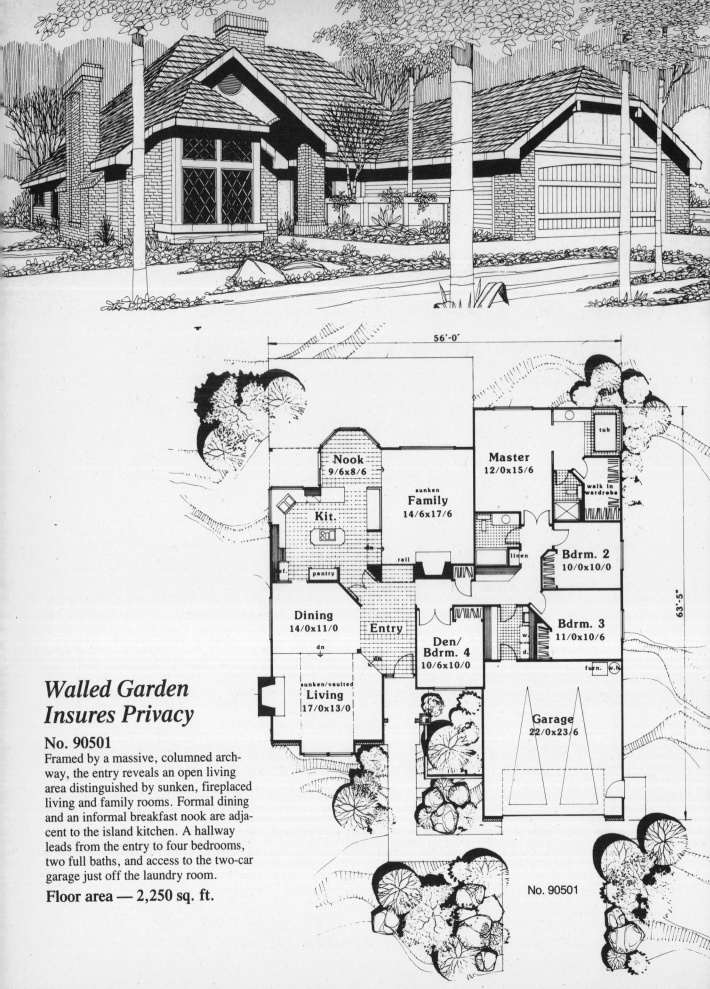

Nook
9/6x8/6

Kit.

pantry

Dining
14/0x11/0

Entry

Master
12/0x15/6

sunken
Family
14/6x17/6

walk in
wardrobe

rail

linen

Bdrm. 2
10/0x10/0

Den/
Bdrm. 4
10/6x10/0

Bdrm. 3
11/0x10/0

furn.   w.h.

sunken/vaulted
Living
17/0x13/0

Garage
22/0x23/6

56'-0"

63'-5"

tub

Walled Garden Insures Privacy

No. 90501

Framed by a massive, columned arch-
way, the entry reveals an open living
area distinguished by sunken, fireplaced
living and family rooms. Formal dining
and an informal breakfast nook are adjacent to the island kitchen. A hallway
leads from the entry to four bedrooms,
two full baths, and access to the two-car
garage just off the laundry room.

Floor area — 2,250 sq. ft.

No. 90501

Country Comfort

No. 91204

Imagine back yard barbecues on the rear deck off this rambling ranch house. The handy kitchen pass-through will insure that serving the side dishes will be a simple matter. You'll love the convenience of the eat-in country kitchen off the foyer. Want a formal atmosphere? Close off the bustle of mealtime preparation with sliding panels. And, after supper, put up your feet, sit by the fire and enjoy the airy atmosphere that soaring ceilings and sliding glass doors give the sunken great room. Three bedrooms are tucked away from active areas. Look at the master suite. Even the largest wardrobe will fit in those twin walk-in closets!

**Main living area — 1,974 sq. ft.
Garage and storage —
612 sq. ft.**

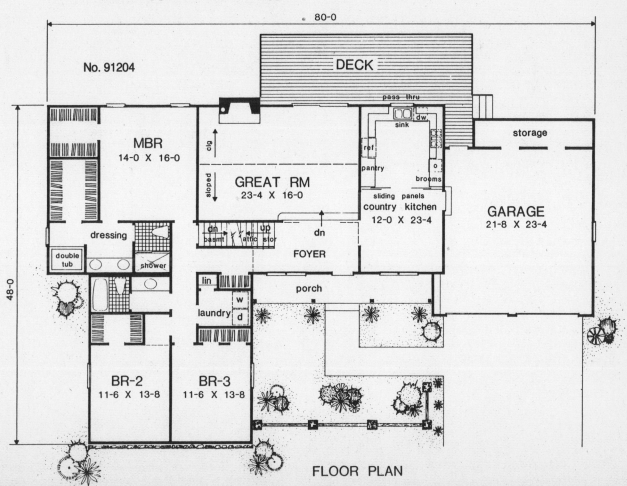

FLOOR PLAN

Privacy Zones

No. 91506

Do you want one-level living without compromising your privacy? Here's a home that will house your family in easy-care elegance, with bedrooms tucked away from the bustle of active areas. The central foyer opens to a large living and dining room combination brightened by a sun-catching bay window. At the rear of the house, an open plan allows the fireplace in the family room to spread its warmth through the angular, efficient kitchen and cheerful nook with sliders to the rear patio. A hallway off the foyer leads to the three bedrooms, laundry room, and handy garage entry. A hall bath serves the kids' rooms, but the master suite features its own private bath with step-in shower.

Main living area — 1,546 sq. ft.
Garage — 2-car

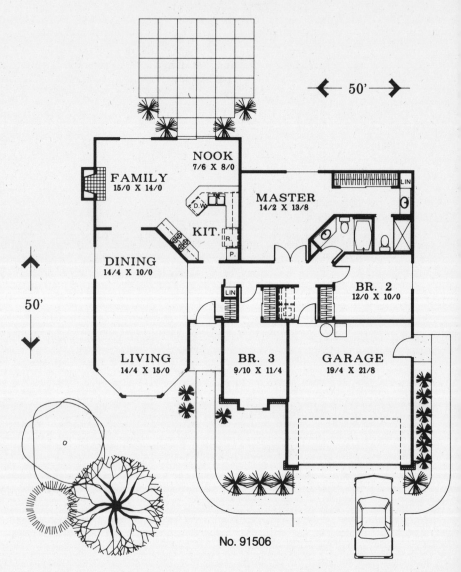

No. 91506

Easy Living

No. 20164

Here's a pretty, one-level home designed for carefree living. The central foyer divides active and quiet areas. Step back to a fireplaced living room with dramatic, towering ceilings and a panoramic view of the backyard. The adjoining dining room features a sloping ceiling crowned by a plant shelf, and sliders to an outdoor deck. Just across the counter, a handy, U-shaped kitchen features abundant cabinets, a window over the sink overlooking the deck, and a walk-in pantry. You'll find three bedrooms tucked off the foyer. Front bedrooms share a handy full bath, but the master suite boasts its own private bath with both shower and tub, a room-sized walk-in closet, and a bump-out window that adds light and space.

Basement — 1,448 sq. ft.
Garage — 452 sq. ft.

Total living area —1,456 sq. ft.

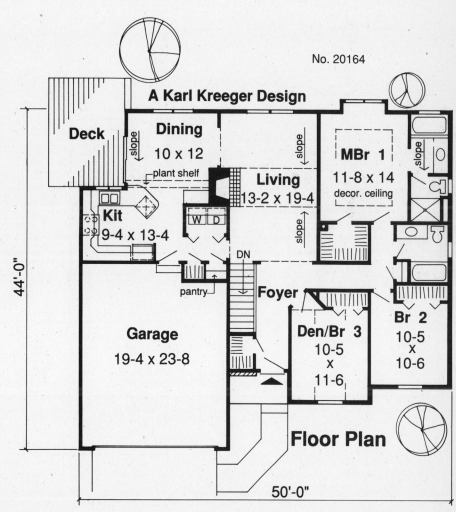

No. 20164

A Karl Kreeger Design

Deck

Dining
10 x 12

plant shelf

Living
13-2 x 19-4

MBr 1
11-8 x 14
decor. ceiling

slope

W D

Kit
9-4 x 13-4

DN

pantry

Foyer

44'-0"

Garage
19-4 x 23-8

Den/Br 3
10-5
x
11-6

Br 2
10-5
x
10-6

Floor Plan

50'-0"

Entrance Court Provides Attractive Focus

No. 90221

Here's one-level living at its best. From bow windows in the spacious living and dining rooms to the master suite with private access to the rear terrace, this attractive, three or four-bedroom home is loaded with elegant appeal. The country kitchen and huge family room share the comfortable warmth of a huge fireplace and rustic, beamed ceilings. Sliders open to the terrace, a perfect spot to enjoy your morning coffee, or an evening of stargazing. Just off the kitchen by the rear entry, the mud and powder rooms provide a handy stopping place for the kids on their way in from an afternoon of play. You'll appreciate the privacy of bedrooms and two full baths well separated from active areas.

**Living area — 1,646 sq. ft.
Garage — 2-car**

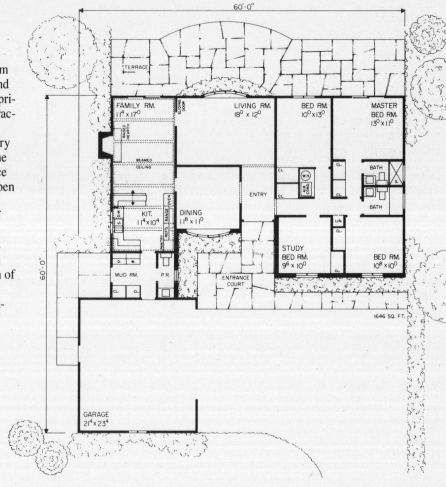

No. 90221

Gardens of the Past

No. 20182

Haven't you always admired the private, walled gardens of English country homes. You can enjoy that and more in this distinctive ranch where central active areas are flanked by private bedroom wings. The central foyer leads three ways: left into the angular kitchen and breakfast room combination, right past the open staircase to a master suite with every amenity, and straight into a huge, fireplaced living room with sloping ceilings, abundant windows, and access to a partially covered wrap-around deck. Step through the elegant, formal dining room with its decorative ceilings and bump-out window to a second bedroom wing. There, you'll find two bedrooms that share full bath overlooking the walled garden.

Basement — 1,930 sq. ft.
Garage — 484 sq. ft.

Total living area — 1,945 sq. ft.

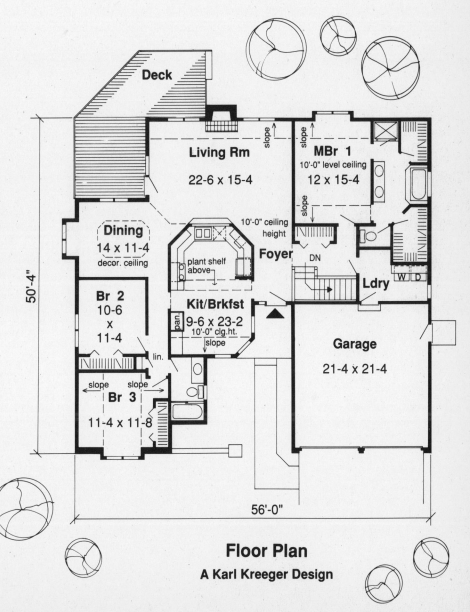

Deck

Living Rm
22-6 x 15-4

MBr 1
10'-0" level ceiling
12 x 15-4

slope

10'-0" ceiling height

Foyer

DN

Dining
14 x 11-4
decor. ceiling

plant shelf above

Ldry
W D

Br 2
10-6
x
11-4

Kit/Brkfst
9-6 x 23-2
10'-0" clg.ht.
slope

pan.

lin.

Garage
21-4 x 21-4

slope   slope

Br 3
11-4 x 11-8

50'-4"

56'-0"

No. 20182

Floor Plan

A Karl Kreeger Design

Arch Recalls Another Era

No. 90675

Massive roof lines pierced with clerestory windows only hint at the interior excitement of this contemporary beauty. The vaulted foyer of this elegant home, graced by doric columns that support an elegant arch, lends an air of ancient Greece to the spacious living and dining rooms. To the right, a well-appointed peninsula kitchen features pass-over convenience to the adjoining dinette bay and family room. Open the sliding glass doors to add an outdoor feeling to every room at the rear of the house. The ample master suite features a private terrace and whirlpool bath. A hall bath serves the other bedrooms in the sleeping wing off the entry.

Main living area — 1,558 sq. ft.
Laundry-mud room — 97 sq. ft.
Garage — 2-car

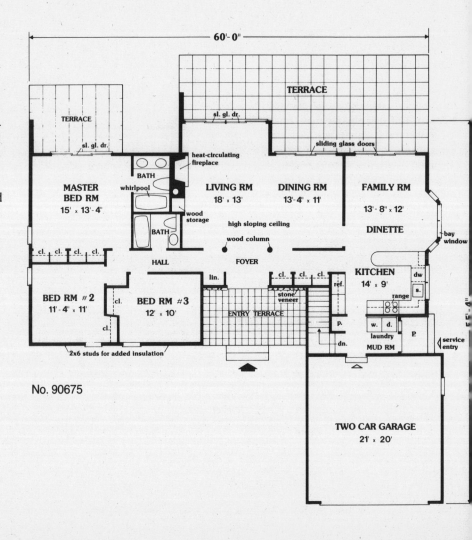

No. 90675

Two-Bedroom Beauty Enjoys Sunny Atmosphere

No. 10773

Here's a compact, one-level home loaded with convenient appeal. Enjoy your morning coffee in the privacy of a sunny breakfast room shielded by a garden wall at the front of the house. The adjoining kitchen also opens to the formal dining room for easy meal times. You'll love the wide-open ambience that flows between dining and sunken, fireplaced living rooms, divided only by a railing and a single step. Sliders to the rear patio accentuate the outdoor feeling. A short hall separates the two bedrooms from active areas, insuring a quiet atmosphere. Imagine the privacy of your own master suite, with a separate entry to the patio, its own full bath, and three roomy closets.

First floor — 1,308 sq. ft.
Garage — one-car

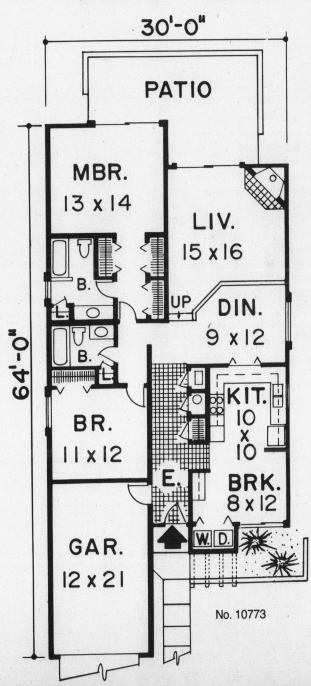

Family Favorite

No. 91415

Active areas surround the island kitchen of this one-level gem designed for convenient family living. Whether you're snacking in the fireplaced family room, having coffee in the sunroom, or serving a formal supper in the dining room, the kitchen is only steps away. Active areas share an expansive view of the backyard, along with three-way patio access. You'll find the master suite tucked behind double doors off the foyer. You'll appreciate the privacy of your own bath with double vanities, a garden tub, and step-in shower. Three bedrooms, another full bath, and a den lie behind the garage for a quiet bedtime atmosphere.

Main living area — 2,706 sq. ft.
Garage — 3-car

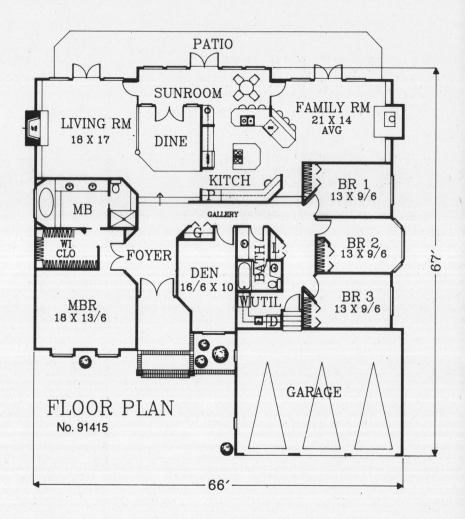

FLOOR PLAN
No. 91415

Master Suite in a Private Wing

No. 90576

Select a carefree home with Southwestern flair. This three-bedroom beauty adapts to any climate, with its shady covered porch and large overhangs to temper the hot summer sun; a vaulted entry, open plan, and abundant windows for excellent air circulation; and fireplaces in both the living and sunken family rooms

to take the winter chill away. The entry offers access to every part of the house. The sunny den and living room lie just inside the front door. The luxury master suite, dining room and informal area including the island kitchen, bay dining nook, and sunken family room span the rear of the house. Two bedrooms, the laundry room, and a full bath are tucked down a short hall just behind the garage.

**Total living area — 2,684 sq. ft.
Garage — 3-car**

79'-1"

76'-7"

tub

Master
16/0x13/6

Dining
12/0x12/0

ref.

Nook
9/6x10/0

dn

sunken
Family
12/6x17/0

desk

pan.

Br. 2
12/6x11/0

linen

Living
17/0x13/0

vaulted
Entry

Br. 3
11/0x11/6

w. d

Den
11/6x12/0

f. wh

Garage
31/0x23/0

No. 90576

Soaring Ceilings, Multiple Levels Add Contemporary Flair

No. 90270

Do you have a lot with a great view? Here's a home with a wide-open feeling that will take advantage of that attractive location. Look at the windows and sliding glass doors linking every room with the great outdoors. The central entry divides the home into active and quiet areas. Three bedrooms and two full baths include the master suite with raised tub, step in shower, and private terrace entrance. Railings separate the massive gathering-dining room from the entry hall. And, when there's a chill in the air, the open arrangement allows every room to benefit from the warmth of the family room fireplace. The efficient island kitchen adjoining the informal eating nook completes an efficient home your family will love.

**Main living area — 2,652 sq. ft.
Garage — 2-car**

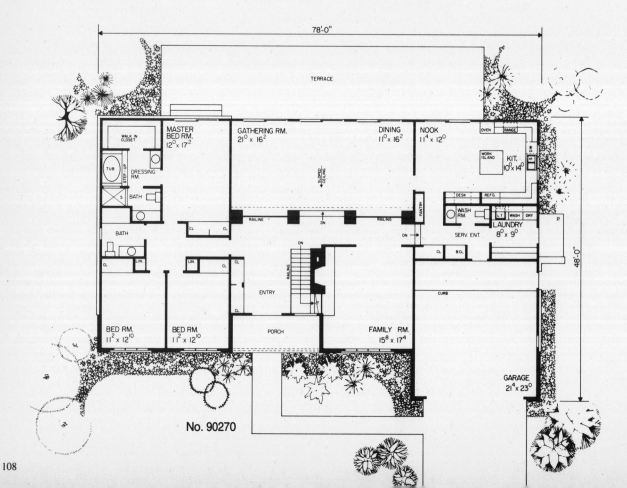

No. 90270

Expansive, Not Expensive

No. 90623

Despite its compact area, this home looks and lives like a luxurious ranch. A decorative screen divides the entrance foyer from the spacious, comfortable living room, which flows into the pleasant dining room overlooking a rear garden. The roomy, eat-in kitchen features a planning corner. And, the adjacent laundry-mud-room provides access to the two-car garage and to the outdoors. Here also lie the stairs to the full basement, a valuable, functional part of the house which adds many possibilities for informal family living. The private bedroom wing includes three bedrooms and two baths.

Total living area — 1,370 sq. ft.

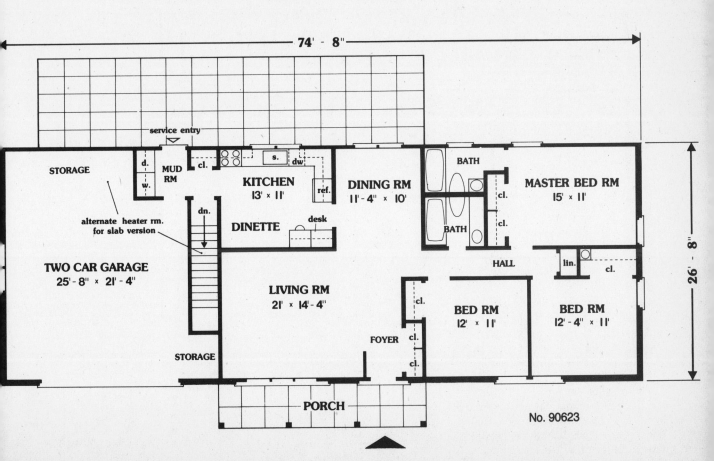

74' - 8"

26' - 8"

service entry

STORAGE

d. w.

MUD RM

cl.

KITCHEN
13' × 11'

s.   dw

ref.

DINING RM
11' - 4" × 10'

BATH

cl.

BATH

cl.

MASTER BED RM
15' × 11'

alternate heater rm.
for slab version

dn.

DINETTE

desk

HALL

lin.

cl.

TWO CAR GARAGE
25' - 8" × 21' - 4"

LIVING RM
21' × 14' - 4"

cl.

BED RM
12' × 11'

BED RM
12' - 4" × 11'

STORAGE

FOYER

cl.

cl.

PORCH

No. 90623

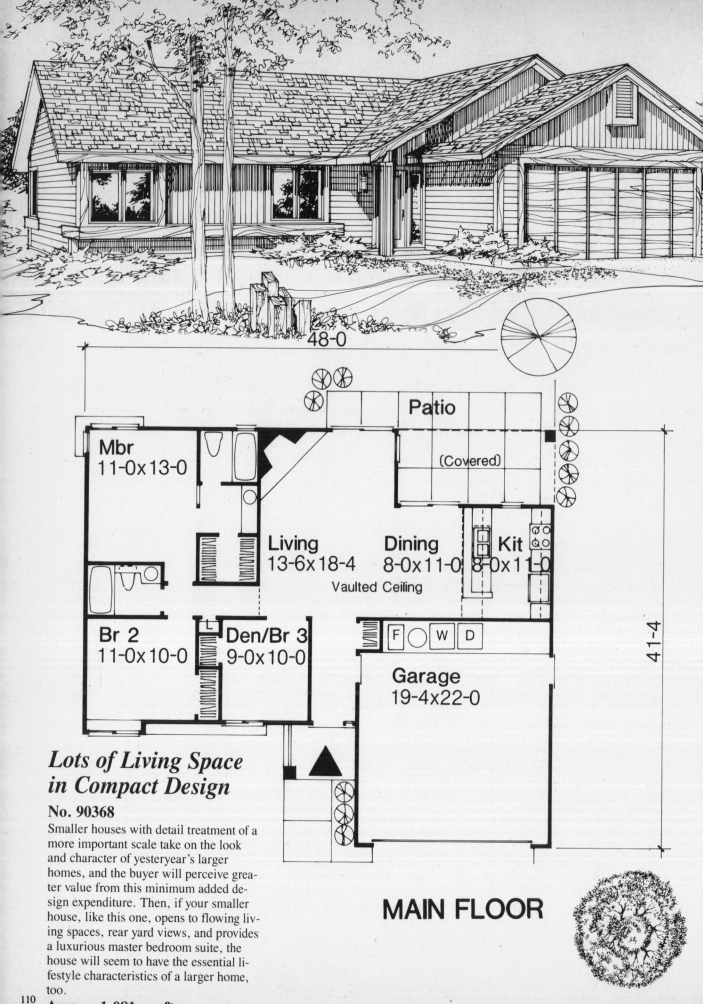

Mbr
11-0x13-0

Living
13-6x18-4
Vaulted Ceiling

Dining
8-0x11-0

Kit
8-0x11-0

Patio

(Covered)

48-0

41-4

Br 2
11-0x10-0

Den/Br 3
9-0x10-0

F W D

Garage
19-4x22-0

Lots of Living Space in Compact Design

No. 90368

Smaller houses with detail treatment of a more important scale take on the look and character of yesteryear's larger homes, and the buyer will perceive greater value from this minimum added design expenditure. Then, if your smaller house, like this one, opens to flowing living spaces, rear yard views, and provides a luxurious master bedroom suite, the house will seem to have the essential lifestyle characteristics of a larger home, too.

MAIN FLOOR

110

Area — 1,081 sq. ft.

Spacious Step-Saver

No. 20145

Classic accents and abundant, well-placed windows give this one-level gem a sunny character all its own. It's hard to decide the living room's best features — the arching, triple window, the dramatic angles of the sloping ceilings, or the two-way fireplace that separates it from the formal dining room overlooking the backyard. A short hall leads to two bedrooms linked by an adjoining full bath. Step past the stairs for a look at the charming, skylit breakfast nook flanked by an outdoor deck and an L-shaped kitchen with step-in pantry. You'll find the master suite, which features a his-and-hers walk-in closet and well-appointed bath, tucked behind the garage for privacy.

Basement — 1,812 sq. ft.

Garage — 484 sq. ft.

Total living area — 1,830 sq. ft.

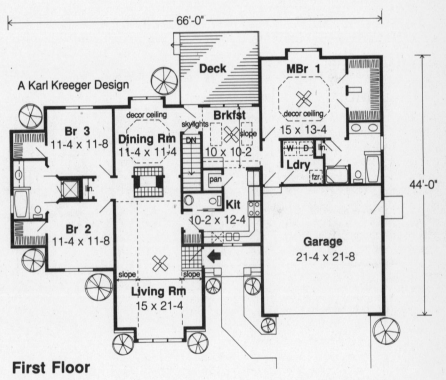

A Karl Kreeger Design

66'-0"

44'-0"

Deck

MBr 1
decor ceiling.
15 x 13-4

Br 3
11-4 x 11-8

Dining Rm
11-4 x 11-4

Brkfst
skylights
10 x 10-2

Ldry
W D lin.
fzr.

Kit
10-2 x 12-4
pan

Br 2
11-4 x 11-8

Garage
21-4 x 21-8

Living Rm
15 x 21-4
slope

First Floor

No. 20145

Unusual Design Creates Comfortable Living

No. 26760

The central focus of this highly pleasing 3 bedroom rancher is the family room, its largest most architecturally interesting space. The first room seen upon entering, this room features a prow shape, a beamed ceiling and a fireplace. Sliding glass doors give access to the multi-leveled deck. The well designed kitchen has a center work island and a large breakfast area overlooking the deck. The dining room and the living room are conveniently placed for ease of entertaining. The master bedroom has a private bath and dressing room. Also included are plenty of closets and a private deck. Two smaller bedrooms share a spacious bath.

Living area — 2,023 sq. ft.
Decks — 589 sq. ft.
Outdoor storage — 36 sq. ft.

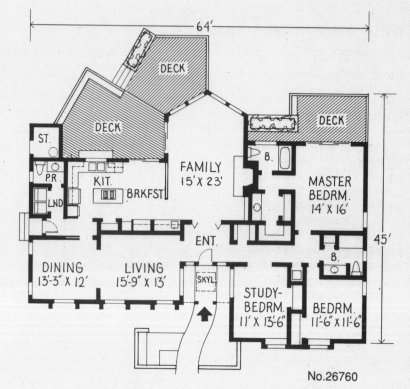

No. 26760

Long, Lean, and Luxurious

No. 90262

The magnificent layout of this modern, three-bedroom plan is very easy to get used to, and difficult to equal. From the three-car garage to the family garden tub surrounded by a privacy wall, this house has all the amenities you've been seeking in a contemporary home. The central entry opens three ways: to the well-appointed meal preparation and dining areas, to the glass-walled gathering room with built-in bar and two-way fireplace, and a few steps down to the bedroom wing. Notice the built-ins throughout this home: the cooktop island and pantry in the kitchen, the planning desk in the breakfast room, and the cabinetry in the study and bedroom closets. A covered porch and terrace add outdoor living space at the rear of the house.

Main living area — 2,732 sq. ft.
Garage — 3-car

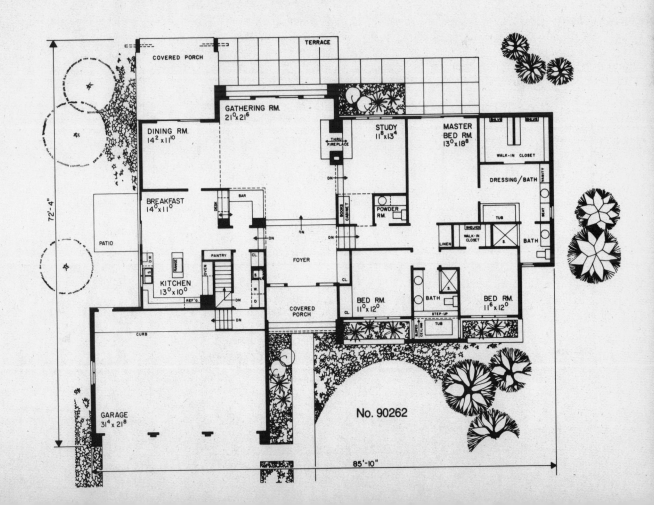

Terrace Doubles Outdoor Living Space

No. 90683

Here's a charming ranch that is loaded with amenities for today's busy family. A covered porch lends a welcoming touch to this compact, yet spacious home adorned with a wood and stone exterior.

A heat circulating fireplace makes the living room a comfortable, cozy place for relaxing. Family areas enjoy an airy greenhouse atmosphere, with three sky-lights piercing the high, sloping ceilings of this wide-open space. A glass wall and sliders to the terrace add to the outdoor feeling. You'll appreciate the pass-over convenience of the side-by-side kitchen

and dining room. And, you'll love the private master suite at the far end of the bedroom wing, with its bay window seat and private bath.

Main living area — 1,498 sq. ft.
Mudroom-laundry — 69 sq. ft.
Basement — 1,413 sq. ft.
Garage — 490 sq. ft.

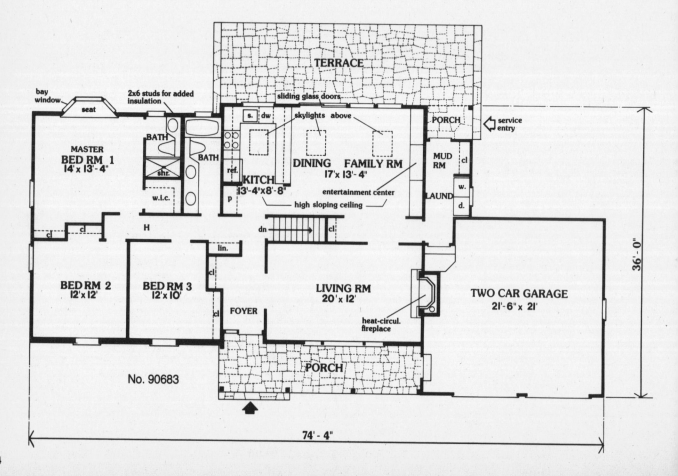

Home Recalls the South

No. 9850

Magnificent white columns, shutters, and small paned windows combine to create images of the antebellum South in this generously proportioned design. Inside, the opulent master bedroom suite, with plentiful closet space, a full bath and study, suggests modern luxury. Fireplaces enhance the formal living room and sizable family room, which skirts the lovely screened porch. The formal dining room boasts built-in china closets.

Basement — 1,447 sq. ft.
Garage — 664 sq. ft.

Total living area — 2,466 sq. ft.

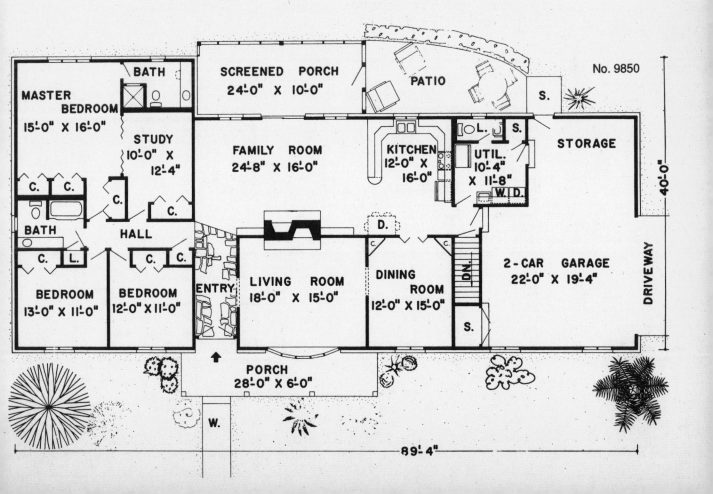

True French Provincial Features Four Bedrooms

No. 90408

This French Provincial design features a master suite with a spacious deluxe bath that includes a garden tub, shower, linen closet, double vanity and large walk-in closets share a second compartmentalized bath. Living and dining rooms are located to the side of the formal foyer. Both the family room, with fireplace and double doors opening onto a screened-in back porch, and a U-shaped kitchen, with an island counter open to the breakfast bay, allow more casual living. Fixed stairs in the family room provide access to attic storage above. Also included is a utility room with a half bath.

Area — 2,968 sq. ft.

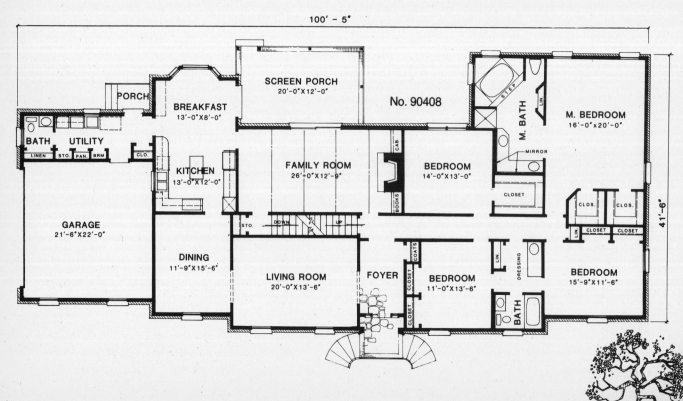

Clutter, Media Rooms Are Uncommon Assets

No. 90294

The cheerful appeal of this contemporary, one-level suncatcher is matched only by its incredible efficiency. The central foyer provides easy access to every area. To the right, you'll find three bedrooms and two full baths, including his and hers walk-in closets, garden whirlpool tub, and private terrace access in the master suite. Soaring living and dining room ceilings add drama to this wide-open area overlooking the terrace. Imagine relaxing in your fully-equipped media room, steps away from the popcorn maker! The country kitchen basks in the warmth of a fireplace and a glass-walled greenhouse, and features pass-through service for easy mealtimes. The clutter room tucked behind the garage provides that handy working space you've always wanted in a home.

Main living area — 2,758 sq. ft.
Garage — 2-car

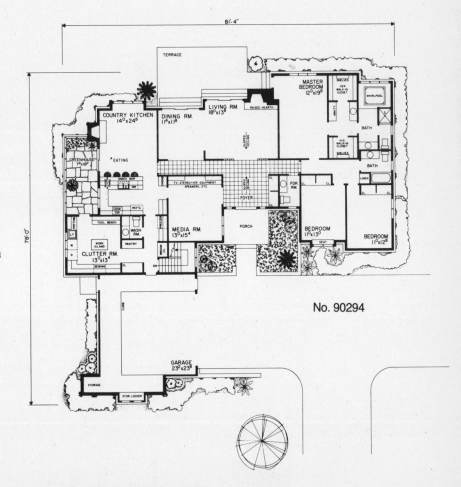

No. 90294

FRONT ELEVATION

Passive Solar With Sun Room

No. 90417

This ranch design features large areas of glass in the master suite and kitchen, and a sun room accessible from both the family room and breakfast room. A recessed entry and a limited amount of glass on the north wall help keep the warm air in during the winter, and over-heating during the summer months is prevented by eliminating glass from the east and west walls. The master suite features a walk-in closet and a compartmentalized bath with linen closet, a second walk-in closet and a dressing area with double vanity. One of the two front bedrooms has a double closet and direct access to a second full bath and the other has a walk-in-closet. A centrally located utility closet and two hall closets complete the left wing. Separating the sunken living room and the foyer area is a massive stone fireplace. A formal dining room can be entered from either the living room or the kitchen. The U-shaped kitchen has a bar counter open to the breakfast area and a mud room with coat closet and access to the garage which acts as a buffer from northwestern winter winds.

Area — 1,859 sq. ft.

FLOOR PLAN

67' 2"

50' 0"

SUN ROOM

PATIO

BREAKFAST
9'-10" x 10'-0"

KITCHEN

MASTER BEDROOM
20'-4" x 15'-6"

DRESS

LIVING ROOM
18'-6" x 17'-6"

DINING
10'-6" x 11'-0"

BATH

FOYER

BEDROOM
13'-6" x 12'-0"

BEDROOM
13'-6" x 11'-8"

GARAGE
21'-0" x 21'-0"

SOUTH ELEVATION

Curbside Appeal

No. 90695

The unique placement of the two-car garage gives this one-level gem an appealing shape that will be welcome in any neighborhood. Step inside, and discover an interior plan that sizzles with excitement. From the skylit foyer faced with stone to the expansive, glass-walled living and dining room, this home possesses a quality of light and space that's hard to equal. Even the galley kitchen with dinette is brightened by a skylight and sliders that open to the greenhouse sunroom. The adjoining family room features a built-in media center, as well as sliders and windows overlooking the rear terrace. Three bedrooms and two full baths, tucked down a hallway off the foyer, complete this exceptional home. This plan is available with basement or slab options. Please specify when ordering.

Basement — 1,505 sq.ft.

Garage — 2-car

Total living area — 1,505 sq. ft.

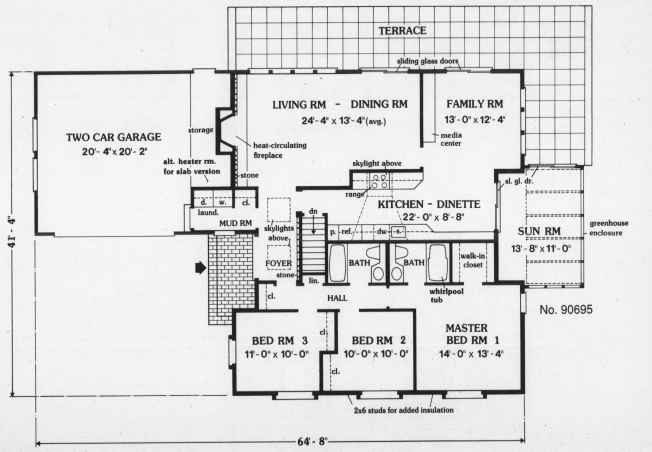

Private Places

No. 90563

The central entry does more than just welcome guests to this spacious, one-level home; it separates active and quiet areas for privacy. In the bedroom wing, you'll find three bedrooms and two full baths. The master suite is a special treat, with its huge, walk-in closet, double vanities, separate toilet area, and jacuzzi tub. The living and dining rooms open to the entry for a wide-open feeling accentuated by towering windows and high ceilings. And, overlooking the backyard, the kitchen of your dreams features a cooktop island, a bayed breakfast nook, and an adjoining family room complete with a cozy fireplace.

Main living area — 1,990 sq. ft.
Garage — 2-car

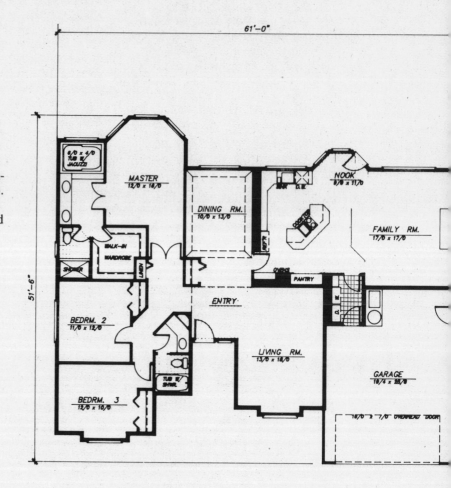

No. 90563

Half-Round Windows and Decorative Shingles

No. 20154

High ceilings in the foyer create a grand entrance for this easy-living ranch whose facade sports half-round windows and decorative shingles. There's lots of room for indoor entertaining in the dramatic sunken living room, created with sloping ceilings and a large fireplace. The kitchen-dining area features a convenient open floor plan, with a bow window and a decorative ceiling adding light and flair. And outdoor entertaining is just a step away on the deck reached through the dining area. The master bedroom also has an ornamental ceiling and offers a large walk-in closet and bath. The remaining two bedrooms share a chic skylit bath with plant shelf.

Basement — 1,392 sq. ft.
Garage — 442 sq. ft.

Total living area — 1,420 sq. ft.

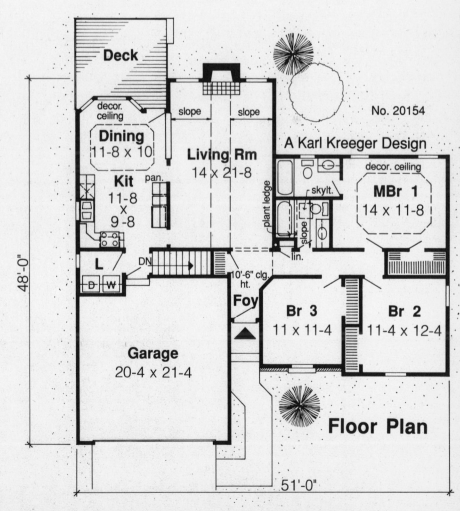

Deck

decor. ceiling

Dining
11-8 x 10

slope   slope

Living Rm
14 x 21-8

No. 20154

A Karl Kreeger Design

Kit
11-8 x 9-8

pan.

decor. ceiling

skylt.

MBr 1
14 x 11-8

plant ledge

L

D   W

DN

slope

lin.

10'-6" clg. ht.

Foy

Br 3
11 x 11-4

Br 2
11-4 x 12-4

48'-0"

Garage
20-4 x 21-4

Floor Plan

51'-0"

One-Level Living with a Twist

No. 20083

Here's an inviting home with a distinctive difference. Active living areas are wide-open and centrally located. From the foyer, you'll enjoy a full view of the spacious dining, living, and kitchen areas in one sweeping glance. You can even see the deck adjoining the breakfast room. The difference in this house lies in the bedrooms. Each is a private retreat, away from active areas. The master suite at the rear of the house features a full bath with double sinks. Two additional bedrooms, off in their own wing, share a full bath and the quiet atmosphere that results from intelligent design.

First floor — 1,575 sq. ft.
Basement — 1,575 sq. ft.
Garage — 475 sq. ft.

A Karl Kreeger Design

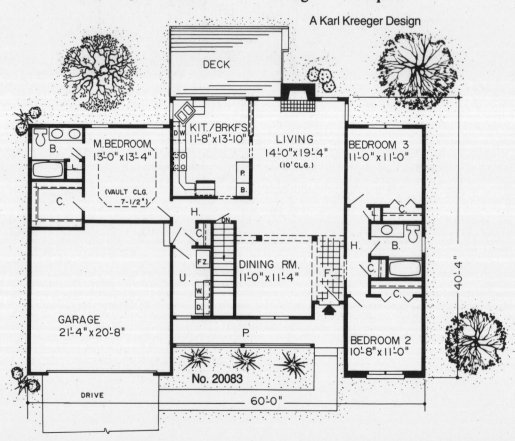

Built-In Beauty

No. 91507

From its skylit foyer to the garden spa in the master suite, this carefree home possesses a sunny charm you'll love coming home to. The living room features a bump-out window that enhances its wide-open arrangement with the formal dining room. At the rear of the house, the efficient island kitchen combines with a cheerful dining nook and fireplaced family room for a spacious, comfortable area just perfect for informal get-togethers. Down a short hall off the foyer, two bedrooms and a full bath flank the laundry room and handy garage entry. The master suite lies behind elegant double doors, boasting a luxurious, private bath with every amenity.

Main living area — 1,687 sq. ft.
Garage — 2-car

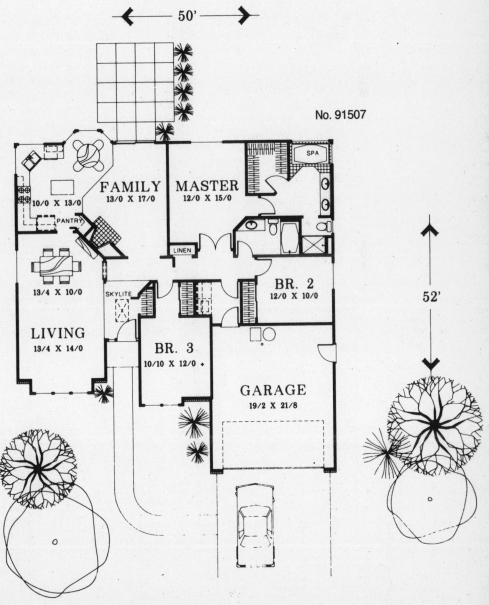

No. 91507

50'

52'

FAMILY
13/0 X 17/0

MASTER
12/0 X 15/0

SPA

PANTRY

LINEN

13/4 X 10/0

BR. 2
12/0 X 10/0

SKYLITE

LIVING
13/4 X 14/0

BR. 3
10/10 X 12/0

GARAGE
19/2 X 21/8

Early American Home for Today

No. 90605

This house reflects the charm and warmth that was prevalent in the early American home 200 years ago. The shuttered, double-hung windows, the moldings at the eaves, the large chimney, and the clapboard siding are elements that capture a colonial flavor. This is reflected in the interior, especially in the "Keeping Room", the early American family gathering place. Located to the rear of the living room, it's used for dining, cooking, and family fun. A counter-height fireplace, pegged plank flooring, beamed ceiling, and colonial-style kitchen cabinets continue the early American motif.

Total living area — 1,260 sq. ft. (optional slab construction available)

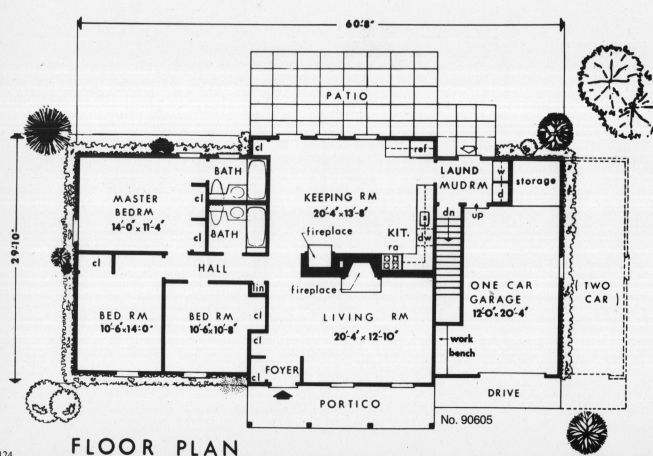

FLOOR PLAN

Detailed Ranch Design

No. 90360

Stylish houses, to suit the higher design expectations of the sophisticated first-time and move-up buyers, need to present a lot of visible values. Starting with the very modern exterior look of this home with its arcaded living room sash, through its interior vaulted spaces and interesting master bedroom suite, this house says "buy me". Foundation offsets are kept to the front where they count for character; simple main roof frames over main house body and master bedroom are cantilevered. Note, too, the easy option of eliminating the third bedroom closet and opening this room to the kitchen as a family room plus two bedroom home.

Main level — 1,283 sq. ft.

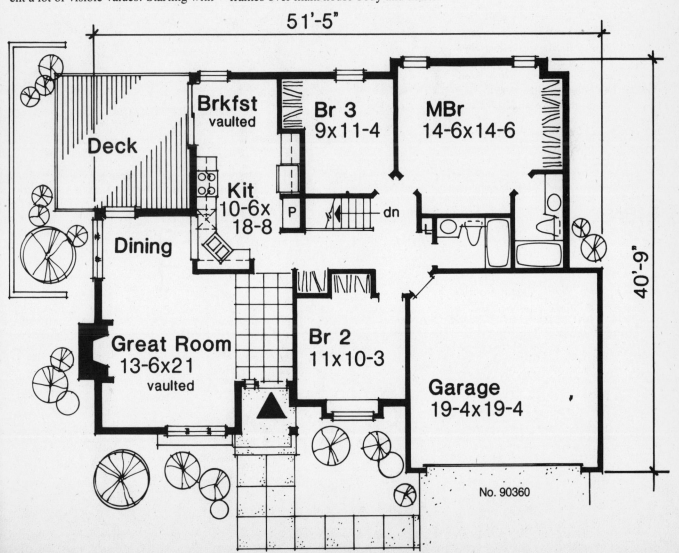

51'-5"

40'-9"

Deck

Brkfst
vaulted

Br 3
9x11-4

MBr
14-6x14-6

Kit
10-6x
18-8

P

dn

Dining

Great Room
13-6x21
vaulted

Br 2
11x10-3

Garage
19-4x19-4

No. 90360

Compact Home for a Small Space

No. 90500

A massive bay window is the dominant feature in the facade of this cozy home with attached two-car garage. From the entry, there are three ways to walk. Turn left into the fireplaced living room and adjoining dining room. Or walk straight into the kitchen and breakfast nook, which extends to a covered porch. Step down the hall on the right to the master suite, full bath, and a second bedroom. The TV room, which can double as a third bedroom, completes the circular floor plan in this convenient, one-level abode.

Floor area — 1,299 sq. ft.

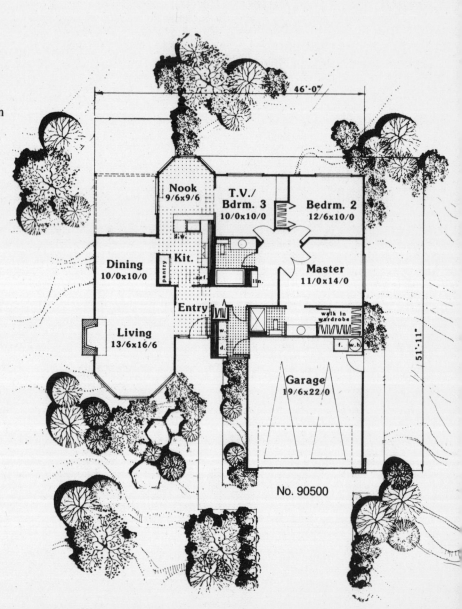

Nook 9/6x9/6

T.V./ Bdrm. 3 10/0x10/0

Bedrm. 2 12/6x10/0

Dining 10/0x10/0

Kit.

pantry

Master 11/0x14/0

Entry

walk in wardrobe

Living 13/6x16/6

Garage 19/6x22/0

46'-0"

51'-11"

No. 90500

Formal Balance

No. 90689

Here's a magnificent example of classical design with a contemporary twist. The graceful columns that adorn the facade of this one-level beauty separate interior spaces without walls. And, combined with the half-round windows in the living room, they create an open, elegant feeling throughout formal areas. A bow window in the dining room overlooking the deck echoes the classic image. Kitchen and dinette share the open atmosphere, flowing together into a spacious unit that opens to the rear deck through sliding glass doors. The master suite enjoys a private corner of the deck, complete with hot-tub, double-vanitied bath, and ample closets. Two front-facing bedrooms across the hall share another full bath.

Main living area — 1,374 sq. ft.
Basement — 1,361 sq. ft.
Mudroom-laundry — 102 sq. ft.
Garage — 548 sq. ft.

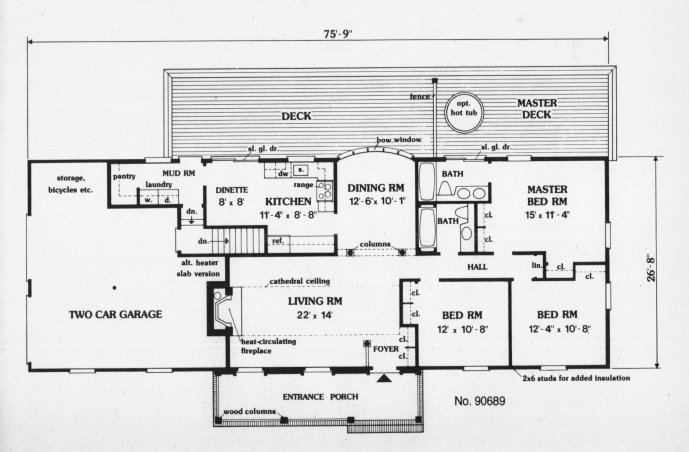

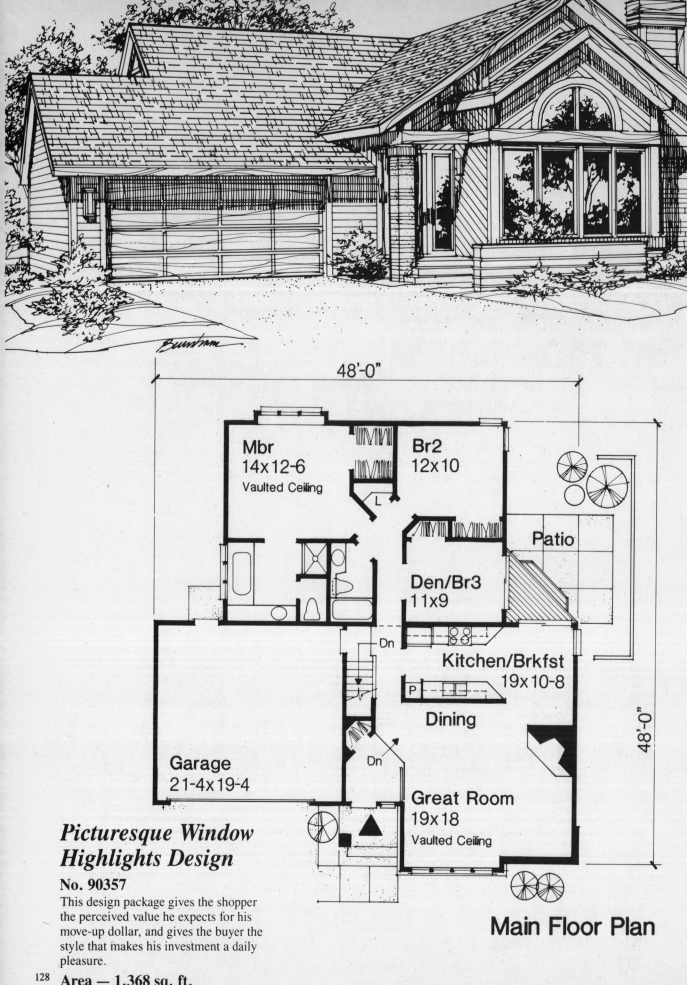

48'-0"

Mbr
14x12-6
Vaulted Ceiling

Br2
12x10

Patio

L

Den/Br3
11x9

Dn

Kitchen/Brkfst
19x10-8

P

Dining

Garage
21-4x19-4

Dn

Great Room
19x18
Vaulted Ceiling

48'-0"

Picturesque Window Highlights Design

No. 90357

This design package gives the shopper the perceived value he expects for his move-up dollar, and gives the buyer the style that makes his investment a daily pleasure.

Main Floor Plan

128 **Area — 1,368 sq. ft.**

Interior and Exterior Unity Distinguishes Plan

No. 90398

Are you a sun worshipper? A rear orientation and a huge, wrap-around deck make this one-level home an outdoor lover's dream. Stepping into the entry, you're afforded a panoramic view of active areas, from the exciting vaulted living room to the angular kitchen overlooking the cheerful breakfast nook. Columns divide the living and dining rooms. Half-walls separate the kitchen and breakfast room. And, the result is a sunny celebration of open space not often found in a one-level home. Bedrooms feature special window treatments and interesting angles. A full bath serves the two front bedrooms, but the luxurious master suite boasts its own private, skylit bath with double vanities, as well as a generous walk-in closet.

Main living area — 1,630 sq. ft.
Garage — 2-car

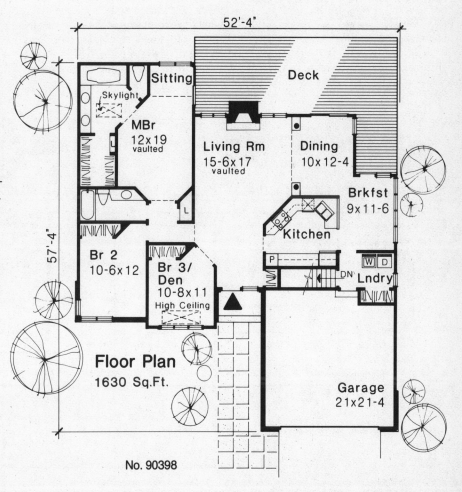

52'-4"

57'-4"

Skylight

Sitting

Deck

MBr
12x19
vaulted

Living Rm
15-6x17
vaulted

Dining
10x12-4

Brkfst
9x11-6

Kitchen

L

Br 2
10-6x12

Br 3/
Den
10-8x11
High Ceiling

P

W D

DN

Lndry

Floor Plan
1630 Sq.Ft.

Garage
21x21-4

No. 90398

Two Fireplaces Provide Warm Appeal

No. 10601

Imagine how impressive this stone exterior and tile roof looks in the morning light. Inside, treat yourself to lavish living. This home is something special with rare features like a parlor and thoughtful touches like the double coat closet in the foyer. The master suite is a knockout with its generous dimensions, walk-in closet, dressing area, deluxe bath, and private door to the patio. This home can accomodate entertaining on any scale thanks to roomy, well defined spaces for the parlor, dining room, living room, den, and family room with wet bar. You'll find all the little extras that make life relaxing.

First floor — 3,025 sq. ft.
Garage — 722 sq. ft.

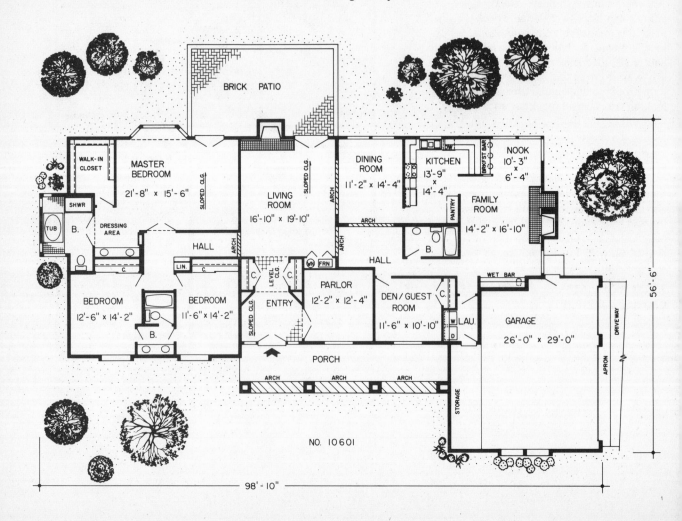

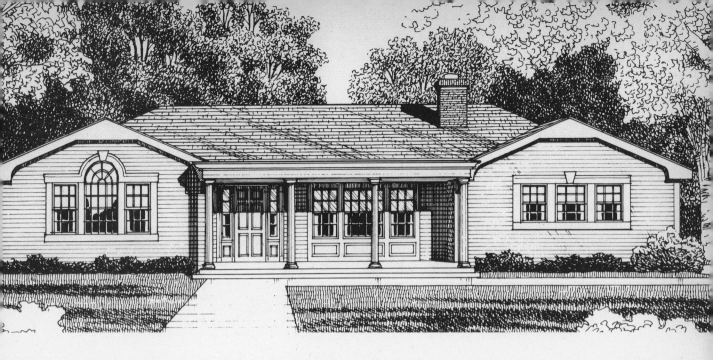

Classic Features

No. 90691

Return to the classics in this carefree ranch. The portico is echoed inside, where columns divide the entry foyer from the dramatic, fireplaced living room. You'll find service and dining areas at the rear of the house, overlooking the terrace. Skylights, a spectacular bow window in the dining room, and sliding glass doors in the country kitchen combine with an open arrangement for an outdoor feeling. The nearby mud and laundry room features two-way access to the garage and the covered side porch. Three bedrooms are tucked away from active areas. A hall bath serves the rear bedrooms, but the master suite boasts a private bath with relaxing whirlpool tub.

Basement — 1,397 sq. ft.
Garage — 2-car

Total living area — 1,397 sq. ft.

No. 90691

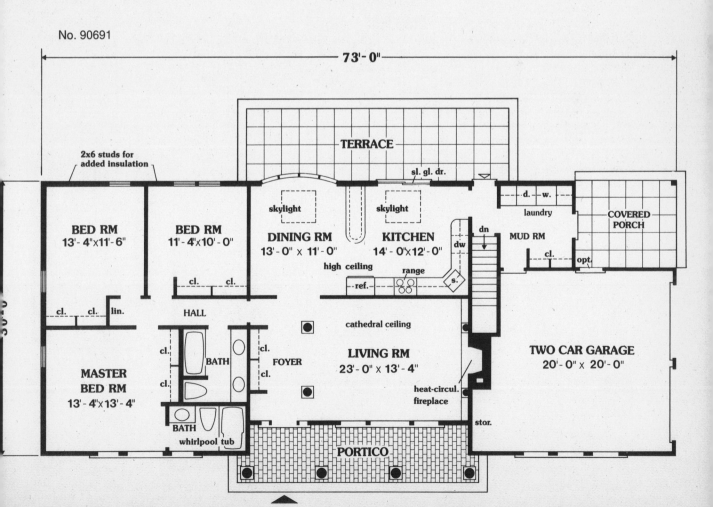

Bump-Out Windows Add Light and Space

No. 20108

Shutters, round-cut shingles, and an attractive railed porch lend classic charm to this three-bedroom home. But this traditional exterior houses an open, updated interior designed for privacy and convenience. A central entry leads three ways: into the formal living room, past the open stairs to a huge, sunny family room crowned by a fireplace, and down an L-shaped hall to the bedroom wing, which includes two full baths. Notice the elegant ceiling treatment and room-size walk-in closet in the master suite. The kitchen is a gourmet's dream, with its range-top island, bump-out window perfect for an indoor herb garden, and strategic location between family and dining rooms.

Main living area — 2,120 sq. ft.
Basement — 2,120 sq. ft.
Garage — 576 sq. ft.

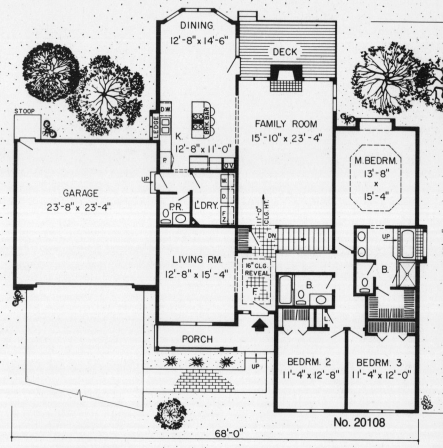

A Karl Kreeger Design

Light and Airy

No. 10745

Diagonal siding accentuates the multiple roof lines in this airy, three-bedroom beauty. Standing in the foyer, you can glance down the stairs that lead to a full basement, or let your eye follow the soaring ceiling to its peak over the kitchen, great room and dining room. The open plan and cathedral ceilings give living areas a spacious feeling. And, with the added outdoor living space the rear deck provides, you'll have plenty of room for entertaining. When your arms are full of groceries, you'll appreciate the convenience of the pantry located just off the garage entry. And, you'll also enjoy the quiet atmosphere in the bedrooms, tucked away in their own wing for maximum privacy.

Main living area — 1,643 sq. ft.
Basement — 1,643 sq. ft.
Garage — 484 sq. ft.

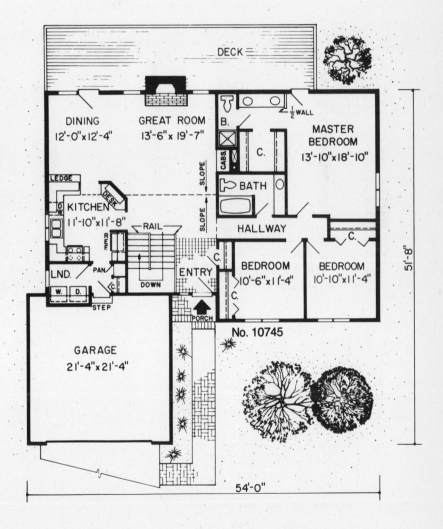

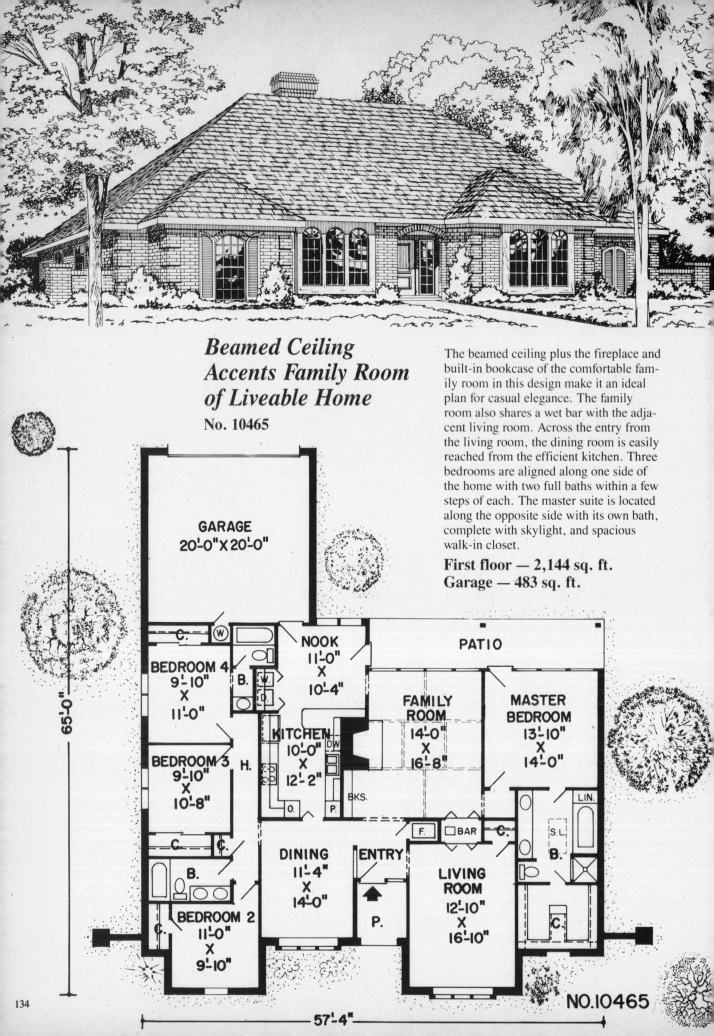

Beamed Ceiling Accents Family Room of Liveable Home

No. 10465

The beamed ceiling plus the fireplace and built-in bookcase of the comfortable family room in this design make it an ideal plan for casual elegance. The family room also shares a wet bar with the adjacent living room. Across the entry from the living room, the dining room is easily reached from the efficient kitchen. Three bedrooms are aligned along one side of the home with two full baths within a few steps of each. The master suite is located along the opposite side with its own bath, complete with skylight, and spacious walk-in closet.

First floor — 2,144 sq. ft.
Garage — 483 sq. ft.

GARAGE
20'-0" X 20'-0"

65'-0"

BEDROOM 4
9'-10"
X
11'-0"

NOOK
11'-0"
X
10'-4"

PATIO

FAMILY
ROOM
14'-0"
X
16'-8"

MASTER
BEDROOM
13'-10"
X
14'-0"

BEDROOM 3
9'-10"
X
10'-8"

KITCHEN
10'-0"
X
12'-2"

LIN.

BKS.

F. BAR

S.L.

DINING
11'-4"
X
14'-0"

ENTRY

LIVING
ROOM
12'-10"
X
16'-10"

BEDROOM 2
11'-0"
X
9'-10"

57'-4"

NO. 10465

Built-ins Add Convenience to Light and Airy One-level

No. 91409

This distinctive one-level design makes maximum use of light and space for an airy atmosphere you'll love. A central foyer separates active and quiet areas.

The skylit bedroom hall leads to two front bedrooms, each with a bump-out window and easy access to a full bath, and the rear master suite. This luxurious retreat features sliding glass doors to a private, covered patio, double vanities, and a huge, sunken tub. Active areas surround the elegant, vaulted dining room, crowned by a skylight. A two-way fireplace separates the soaring living and

family areas. You'll love the spacious family area, which includes a well-equipped kitchen with rangetop island, a sunny eating bay, and family room with patio access. Specify crawlspace or basement when ordering.

Main living area — 2,215 sq. ft.
Garage — 539 sq. ft.

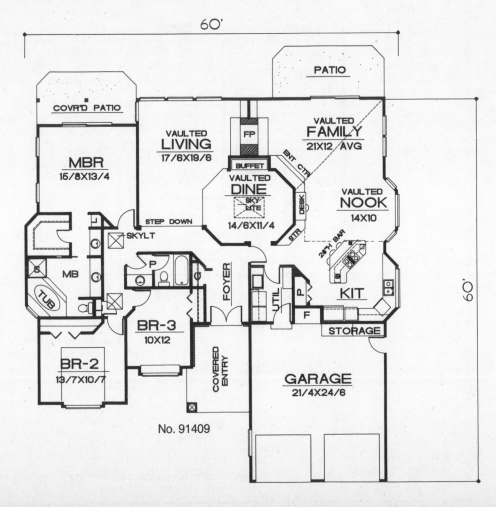

No. 91409

Delightful Doll House

No. 20161

With its railed porch and gingerbread trim, this convenient ranch looks like a Victorian doll house. But there's lots of room in this compact, three-bedroom plan. The foyer, tucked between the two-car garage and bedroom wing, opens to a spacious, fireplaced living room. Soaring ceilings and an open arrangement with the adjoining dining room add to the airy feeling in this sunny space. The kitchen, steps away, offers easy, over-the-counter service at mealtime. And there's a large pantry just across from the adjacent laundry room. The two front bedrooms share a full bath. The master suite boasts its own private bath, plus a closet-lined wall and decorative touches that make it special.

Basement — 1,298 sq. ft.
Garage — 462 sq. ft.

Total living area — 1,307 sq. ft.

No. 20161

A Karl Kreeger Design

Deck

decor. ceiling
MBr 1
12-8 x 11-4

slope

decor. ceiling
Dining
10 x 11-4

Kit
9-6 x 10

lin.

slope

Living Rm
13 x 19-4

DN

pantry

W
L
D

38'-0"

lin.

opt. door location

Foy

Garage
20-4 x 21-8

Br 3/Den Study
10 x 11-4

Br 2
10-8 x 10-8

Floor Plan

50'-0"

Sunshine Special

No. 20150

Looking for carefree living? This charming, one-level gem fits the bill with three bedrooms, two full baths, and active areas located for convenience. The skylit foyer leads three ways. Step down to an expansive living room, where a towering fireplace accentuates the sloping ceilings, and sliding doors to the patio create an outdoor feeling. Or, walk straight into the well-equipped kitchen, which opens to a bay dining room with four glass walls and an adjoining deck. In the quiet wing to the left, you'll find a walk-in closet in every bedroom, a skylit hall bath, and a spacious master suite with a decorative ceiling and luxury bath.

Basement — 1,320 sq. ft.
Garage — 462 sq. ft.

Total living area — 1,638 sq. ft.

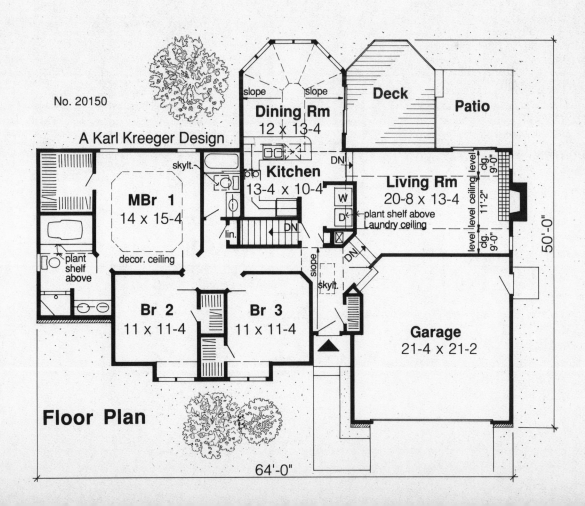

No. 20150

A Karl Kreeger Design

Dining Rm 12 x 13-4
Deck
Patio
slope   slope

skylt.

Kitchen 13-4 x 10-4
Living Rm 20-8 x 13-4

MBr 1 14 x 15-4

plant shelf above

decor. ceiling

lin.

DN

w
D

plant shelf above
Laundry ceiling

level level ceiling level
clg. 11'-2"
clg. 9'-0"
clg. 9'-0"

50'-0"

slope

skylt.

Br 2 11 x 11-4
Br 3 11 x 11-4

Garage 21-4 x 21-2

DN

Floor Plan

64'-0"

Outdoor-Lovers' Delight

No. 90248

If outdoor entertaining is your pleasure, this is the perfect house. Rain or shine, the covered porch off the dining room provides shelter, while the rear terrace lets you have fun in the sun. And, every room enjoys an outdoor atmosphere, thanks to sliding glass doors and over-sized windows. The well-appointed kitchen, centrally located just steps away from formal dinners, family suppers in the breakfast nook, or h'ors doeuvres in the soaring gathering room, is a cook's dream. Three bedrooms, tucked down a hall off the foyer, include the spacious master suite with its own private terrace access and full bath with step-in shower.

Main living area — 1,729 sq. ft.
Garage — 2-car

No. 90248

OPTIONAL NON-BASEMENT

Pretty Palladium

No. 91627

This easy-care home combines classic elements with modern zoning for carefree living on a grand scale. The octagonal great hall directs traffic flow throughout the house: to the front-facing den, to the elegant, coved living room with its triple-arched windows and cozy fireplace, to the informal areas at the rear of the house and the bedroom wing tucked behind the garage. You'll love the gourmet kitchen with its rangetop island overlooking the bay dining nook and coved, fireplaced family room. And, the adjoining rear deck is a nice spot for a warm-weather party. Three bedrooms include an exquisite master suite with private, double-vanitied bath with garden spa, a walk-in closet, and a bay-window view of the backyard. This plan is built on a crawlspace foundation.

Garage — 2-car

Total living area — 2,097 sq. ft.

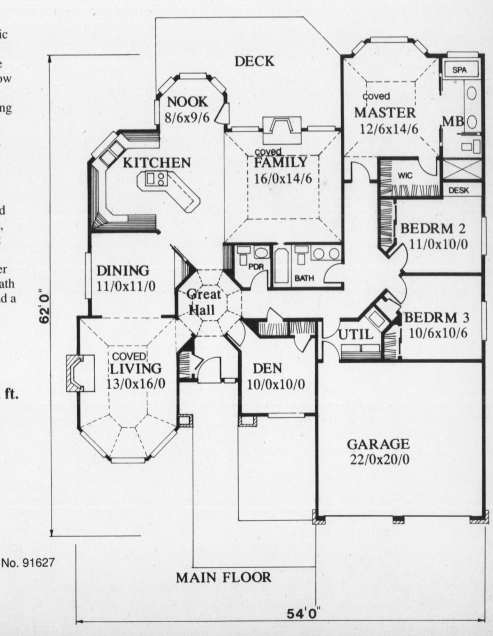

No. 91627

MAIN FLOOR

Master Bedroom Suite Accentuates Luxury

No. 9870

Adorned with pillars and a bow window, this French Provincial design becomes an exercise in elegance, crowned by the master bedroom suite. Placed to allow full privacy, the master bedroom incorporates a segmented bath, large walk-in closet, and sitting room with its own closet. A firelit living room and dining room augment an appealing family room, which opens to the terrace. Beyond the kitchen, a laundry room, half bath, and closet space add to the charm.

First floor — 2,015 sq. ft.
Basement — 2,015 sq. ft.
Garage — 545 sq. ft.

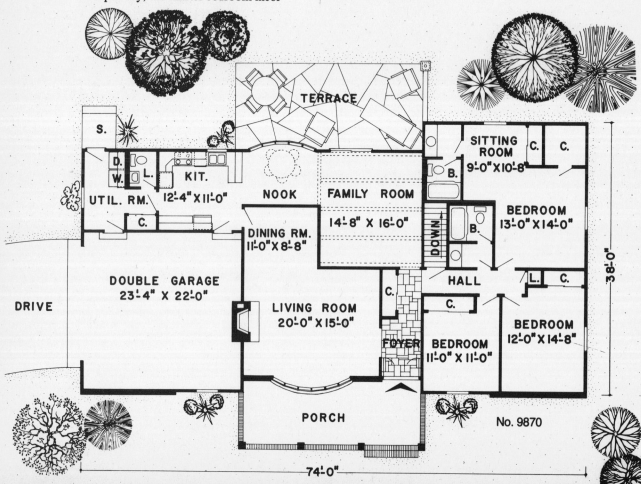

Private Wing Houses Bedrooms

No. 90225

Touches of Tudor styling decorate the facade of this attractive, one-level home. The foyer opens to a large living room with beamed ceilings and a huge fireplace. With the adjoining formal dining room just steps away, this is a magnificent location for entertaining. A sliding door shields guests from the bustle of the busy kitchen. When the occasion calls for relaxation, retire to the cozy family room, which features pass-over convenience to the kitchen, and access to the rear terrace through sliding glass doors. And, there's a handy powder room right around the corner past the laundry. Three bedrooms, tucked away from active areas in their own wing, feature walk-in closets.

Living area — 1,769 sq. ft.
Garage — 2-car

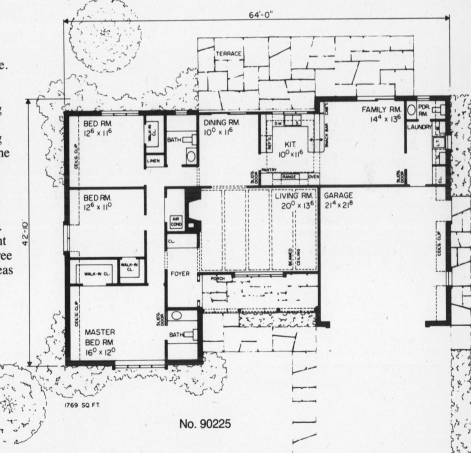

No. 90225

Captivating Sun-Catcher

No. 99303

Can't you imagine spreading out your Sunday paper in the glass-walled breakfast room of this cheerful home? Decorative columns and a half-round window give this sun-filled space a romantic quality that's almost irresistible. And, with an ingenious, wide-open plan, solar warmth circulates throughout active areas, saving on your energy bills. When there's a chill in the air, every room will benefit from the warmth of the fireplace in the vaulted living room. Abundant windows and sliders to a rear deck unite active areas and the master suite with the great outdoors. And, look at the greenhouse window over the tub in the luxurious master bath. Even your plants will appreciate the inviting atmosphere of this compact gem!

Main living area — 1,230 sq. ft.
Garage — 2-car

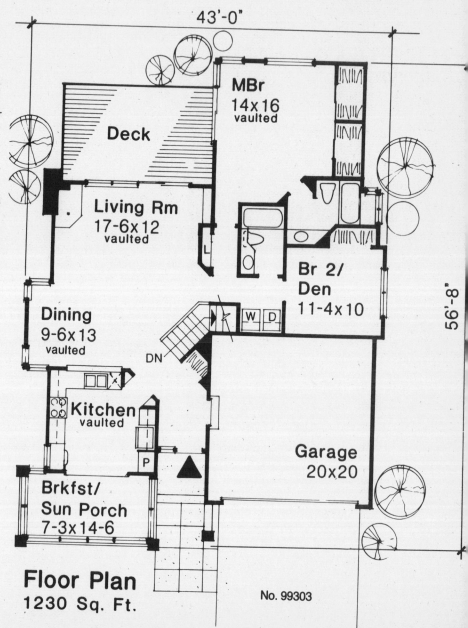

43'-0"

56'-8"

Deck

MBr
14x16
vaulted

Living Rm
17-6x12
vaulted

Br 2/
Den
11-4x10

Dining
9-6x13
vaulted

DN

W D

Kitchen
vaulted

Garage
20x20

P

Brkfst/
Sun Porch
7-3x14-6

Floor Plan
1230 Sq. Ft.

No. 99303

Celebration of Light and Space

No. 91212

Vertical and diagonal siding reinforces the soaring roof lines of this dramatic contemporary. And inside, the excitement of open space and lots of glass insures a sunny atmosphere in any weather. When the sun goes down, the massive fireplace dominating the great room will add a cozy glow. The cook will never be lonely in the efficient island kitchen that easily serves the breakfast bar or the dining room table overlooking the trellissed deck. Large vertical windows and generous closets characterize the three cheerful bedrooms tucked into a private wing. And, look at the sunroom that encloses the tub in the master suite. There's a lot of luxury in this compact home!

Living area — 1,873 sq. ft.
Garage — 467 sq. ft.

No materials list available

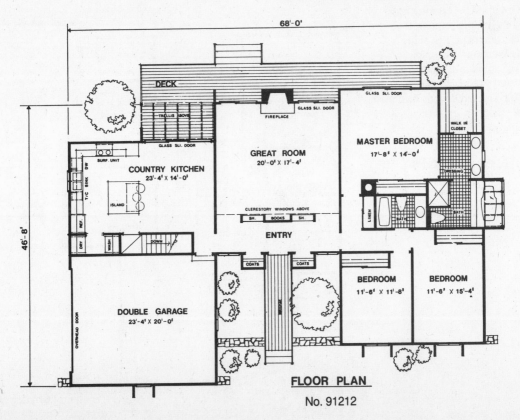

FLOOR PLAN

No. 91212

Stucco Suncatcher

No. 90945

You'll enjoy the sunny, easy-care atmosphere of this handsome, stucco home. An arched window over the vaulted foyer sets the stage for the spaciousness you'll find throughout the house. To the left, the bedroom wing occupies a quiet corner away from the action. The front bedrooms share a vaulted ceiling, each with an arched window, and easy access to the hall bath. The master suite enjoys a private bath and walk-in closet. Active areas include the formal living room overlooking the backyard, and the dining room with corner window treatment, just steps away from the kitchen. The open arrangement of kitchen, fireplaced family room, and glass walled nook surrounding the covered deck is designed for family interaction.

Garage — 2-car

Total living area — 1,963 sq. ft.

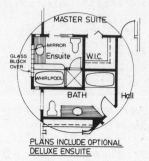

MASTER SUITE

GLASS BLOCK OVER

MIRROR

Ensuite W.I.C.

WHIRLPOOL

BATH Hall

PLANS INCLUDE OPTIONAL DELUXE ENSUITE

No. 90945

MASTER SUITE 15-4 × 12-0

LIVINGROOM 14-0 × 16-0

Gas FP

Sunken FAMILY ROOM 12-0 × 16-0

Covered Deck

NOOK 9-0 × 11-0

ENS. W.I.C.

railing down

railing

dn

BATH towel

Hall

linen

Vaulted clg.

FOYER

KITCHEN 12-0 × 12-0

DW

R

DESK

PANTRY

F

BR 3 11-4 × 9-6/13-4

BR 2 11-4 × 14-6/9-6

DINING 12-0 × 12-0

Lav.

W D

UTILITY

vaulted clg.

DOUBLE GARAGE 23-0 × 23-6

58'-0"

60'-0"

Colonial Ranch Style, Enriched Interior

No. 9864

Endowed with the trimmings of a traditional colonial, this three-bedroom ranch is doubly attractive. The master bedroom is complete with a full bath, walk-in closet and spacious dressing area. Warmed by a wood-burning fireplace, the living room spills onto a large redwood deck via a sliding glass door. A functional kitchen is separated from the family room by a cooking peninsula. A utility room and hobby shop edge the double garage.

First floor — 1,612 sq. ft.
Basement — 1,612 sq. ft.
Garage, utility room and storage — 660 sq. ft.

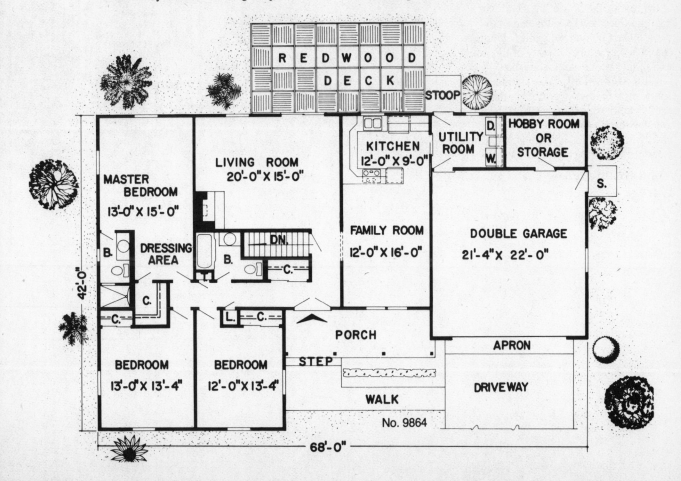

Soaring Spaces

No. 91611

The dramatic roof lines of this one level gem hint at the exciting plan you'll find inside. Step into the foyer, lit from above by a high, arched window, and look into the coved great hall at the center of the house. Surrounded by the fireplaced living room, a sunny den, the distinctive formal dining room, and informal areas at the rear of the house, the great hall also provides access to the bedroom wing tucked behind the garage. Notice the exceptional open quality of the informal family room, nook and island kitchen, warmed by a cozy fireplace and abundant windows overlooking the rear deck. The master suite is special, with its angular shape, walk-in closet, and private bath. And the hall bath is just a step away from the other two bedrooms.

Main living area — 2,352 sq. ft.
Garage — 2-car

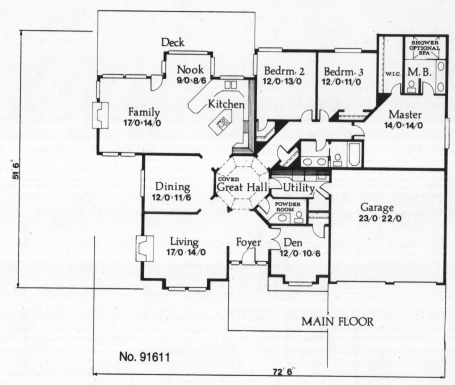

Deck

Nook
9/0×8/6

Kitchen

Family
17/0×14/0

Bedrm. 2
12/0×13/0

Bedrm. 3
12/0×11/0

W.I.C.

SHOWER
OPTIONAL
SPA

M. B.

Master
14/0×14/0

Dining
12/0×11/6

COVED
Great Hall

Utility

POWDER
ROOM

Garage
23/0·22/0

Living
17/0·14/0

Foyer

Den
12/0·10/6

51' 6"

MAIN FLOOR

No. 91611

72' 6"

Hillside Excitement

No. 90541

Have you been searching in vain for a home that will fit your hillside lot? This multi-level wood and brick ranch provides an exciting option you'll want to pursue. Stand in the central hallway, and enjoy the view of the entry and fireplaced living room below. Double doors keep family areas — the expansive island kitchen, bay eating nook, and comfortable family room — separate from the elegant atmosphere of the formal dining room. The bedroom wing is well separated from active areas for maximum privacy. The luxurious master suite features a compartmentalized, double-vanitied bath with a raised tub and step-in shower. The two rear bedrooms share another full bath and a terrific view of the back yard.

Main living area — 2,174 sq. ft.
Garage — 2-car

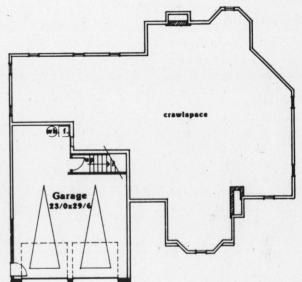

No. 90541

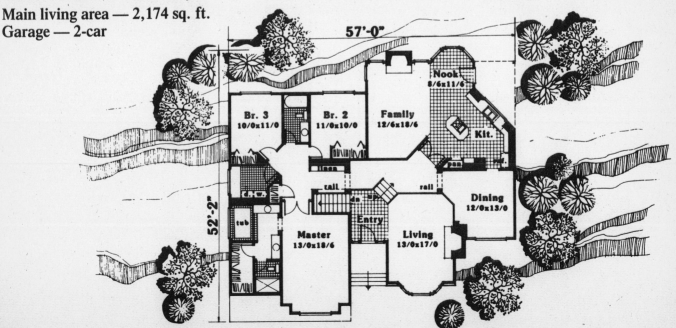

Comfort Zones

No. 90566

Here's a sprawling suncatcher with a distinctive difference — living areas are zoned for convenience. The skylit entry opens four ways: into the sun-filled elegance of the formal living and dining rooms, to the quiet comfort of a book-lined study, to family areas at the rear of the house, and to the bedroom wing tucked behind the garage. The breakfast nook and fireplaced family room wrap around a well-equipped kitchen at the rear of the house. The master suite is a mirror image of family areas, with its bayed sitting area and double-vanitied bath with jacuzzi tub sharing the backyard view. Another full, skylit bath separates the other two bedrooms, located on a hallway leading to the garage.

Main living area — 2,180 sq. ft.
Garage — 2-car

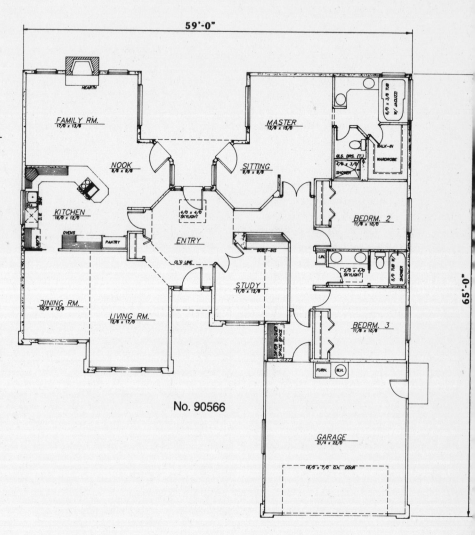

No. 90566

148

Hip Roof Design, Family-centered Space

No. 22008

Inside this trim hip roof plan, space is alloted for a variety of family activities. Spotlighted is the sizable beamed family room with a fireplace and access to the porch. The bordering gameroom edges a handy half bath, and the dining nook connects to, and visually enlarges, the kitchen. Four bedrooms and two full baths are included in this plan.

Living area — 2,074 sq. ft.
Garage — 544 sq. ft.

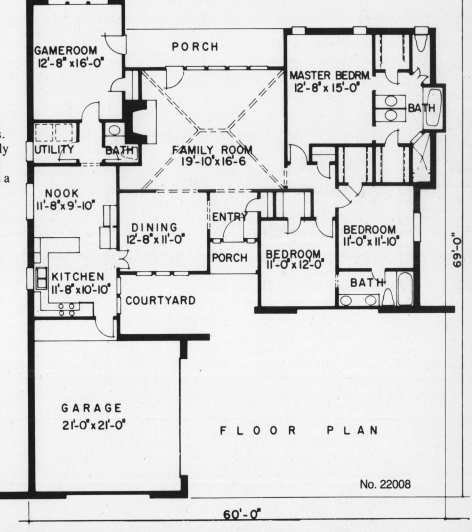

GAMEROOM
12'-8" x 16'-0"

PORCH

MASTER BEDRM.
12'-8" x 15'-0"

BATH

UTILITY

BATH

FAMILY ROOM
19'-10" x 16-6

NOOK
11'-8" x 9'-10"

DINING
12'-8" x 11'-0"

ENTRY

PORCH

BEDROOM
11'-0" x 11'-10"

BEDROOM
11'-0" x 12'-0"

BATH

KITCHEN
11'-8" x 10'-10"

COURTYARD

GARAGE
21'-0" x 21'-0"

FLOOR PLAN

No. 22008

69'-0"

60'-0"

Doubly Warm

No. 20174

You'll feel the cozy atmosphere as soon as you step into the foyer of this one-level charmer. To the right, a formal dining room overlooking the front yard enjoys a convenient location just over the counter from a U-shaped kitchen. Enjoy the warmth of the two-way fireplace here, or in the spacious living room at the rear of the house. High ceilings and the adjoining deck give this attractive room an outdoor feeling. You'll find two bedrooms and a full bath tucked off the foyer. The master suite occupies its own private corner behind the garage. With its sloping ceilings and skylit bath, this quiet retreat possesses a sunny charm of its own.

Basement — 1,538 sq. ft.
Garage — 455 sq. ft.

Total living area — 1,538 sq. ft.

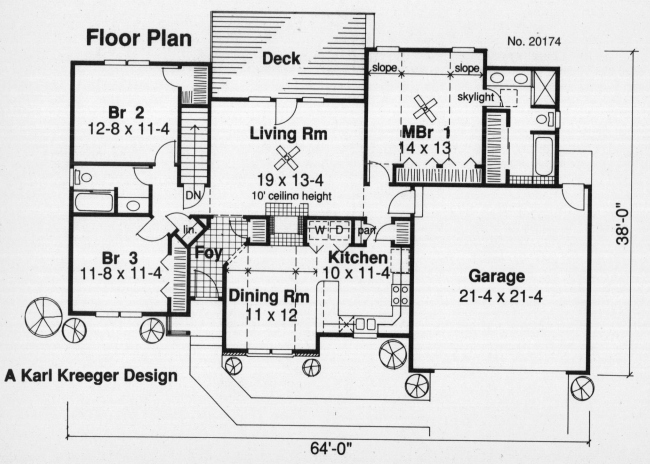

Floor Plan

No. 20174

Deck

Br 2
12-8 x 11-4

Living Rm
19 x 13-4
10' ceiling height

slope   slope
skylight

MBr 1
14 x 13

DN

lin.

Foy

W D pan.

Br 3
11-8 x 11-4

Kitchen
10 x 11-4

Dining Rm
11 x 12

Garage
21-4 x 21-4

38'-0"

64'-0"

A Karl Kreeger Design

150

Classic Arches

No. 20180

Twin-arched windows and a friendly, covered porch accent the brick and clapboard exterior of this convenient, one-level plan. The angled entry adds intrigue to the sunny, soaring kitchen-breakfast room combination. This open arrangement, divided by a rangetop island, features every amenity including a built-in pantry, counter space galore, and a double sink with a view. The living and dining rooms at the rear of the house flow together in one magnificent space accented by high ceilings, abundant windows, and a wrap-around deck that doubles your outdoor living area. In the quiet bedroom wing, the rear-facing master suite features a luxury bath and decorative ceilings. Two more sunny bedrooms lie past the second full bath and convenient laundry.

Basement — 1,579 sq. ft.
Garage — 487 sq. ft.

Total living area —1,592 sq. ft

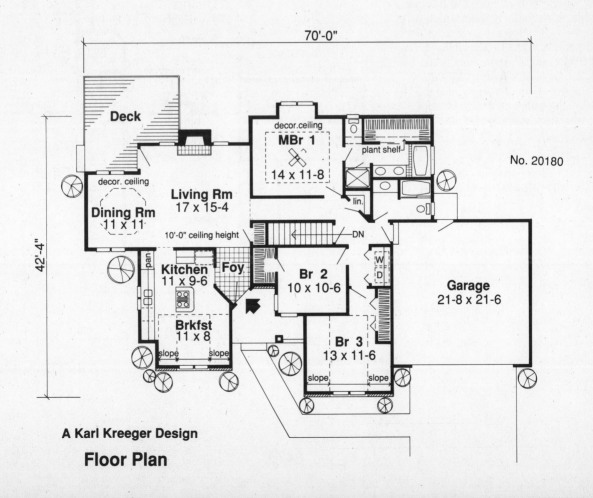

A Karl Kreeger Design

Floor Plan

Georgian Grace

No. 20116

Slender columns and brick detailing lend a Georgian influence to this one-level classic. The entry opens to a formal living room characterized by high ceilings, elegant arched windows, and a cozy fireplace. To the left, a short hall leads to a full bath and two bedrooms, each with a walk-in closet. At the rear of the house, you'll find a large, formal dining room with bay window and sliders to an outdoor deck. The kitchen, just steps away, overlooks the backyard. Past the laundry lies the luxurious master suite. Notice the attractive ceiling treatment, and the adjoining bath with double vanities, step-in shower, and raised tub.

Basement — 1,653 sq. ft.
Garage — 520 sq. ft.

Total living area —1,677 sq. ft.

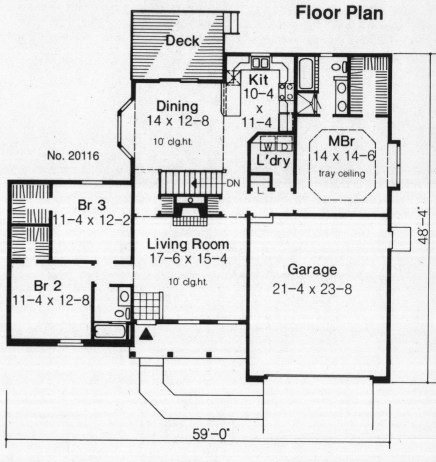

Floor Plan

No. 20116

Deck

Kit
10-4
x
11-4

Dining
14 x 12-8
10' clg.ht.

W D

L'dry

MBr
14 x 14-6
tray ceiling

DN

Br 3
11-4 x 12-2

Living Room
17-6 x 15-4
10' clg.ht.

Garage
21-4 x 23-8

Br 2
11-4 x 12-8

48'-4"

59'-0"

A Karl Kreeger Design

Classic Comforts

No. 20183

You don't have to give up a gracious atmosphere for smart, utilitarian design. This one-level beauty is a perfect combination of elegance and easy-care convenience. Arched windows add romance and drama to both the magnificent master suite and rear-facing breakfast room just over the counter from the well-equipped kitchen. You'll enjoy family meals in this informal, sunny atmosphere, but when you want to entertain in style, choose the formal dining room. A fireplace adds warmth to the spectacular vaulted living room, which features abundant windows overlooking the rear deck and the back yard. Two more bedrooms share a full bath in an ideal location near the laundry room.

Basement — 1,863 sq. ft.
Garage — 508 sq. ft.

Total living area — 1,877 sq. ft.

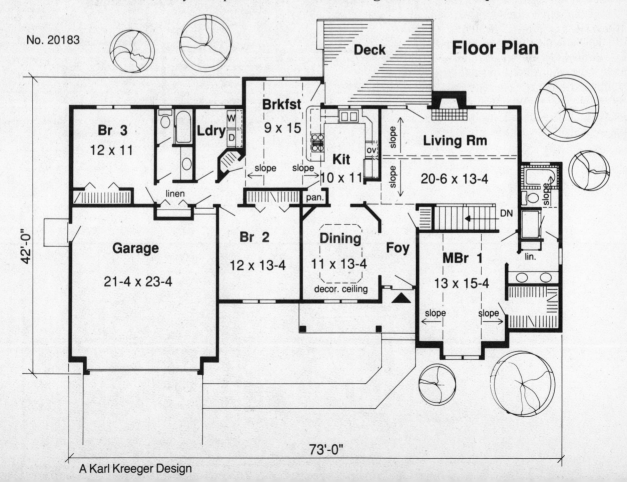

No. 20183

Floor Plan

Deck

Br 3 12 x 11

Ldry

W D

Brkfst 9 x 15

slope

slope

Living Rm 20-6 x 13-4

slope

slope

Kit 10 x 11

ov

linen

pan.

DN

slope

Garage 21-4 x 23-4

Br 2 12 x 13-4

Dining 11 x 13-4

decor. ceiling

Foy

MBr 1 13 x 15-4

lin.

slope

slope

42'-0"

73'-0"

A Karl Kreeger Design

Compact and Appealing

No. 20075

Here's an L-shaped country charmer with a porch that demands a rocking chair or two. You'll appreciate the convenient one-level design that separates active and sleeping areas. Right off the foyer, the formal dining and living rooms have a wide-open feeling, thanks to extra wide doorways and a recessed ceiling. The kitchen is centrally located for maximum convenience. For informal family meals, you'll delight in the sunny breakfast nook that links the fireplaced living room and outdoor deck. Enjoy those quiet hours in the three bedrooms separated from family living spaces. With its own double-sink full bath and walk-in closet, the master suite will be your favorite retreat.

First floor — 1,682 sq. ft.
Basement — 1,682 sq. ft.
Garage — 484 sq. ft.

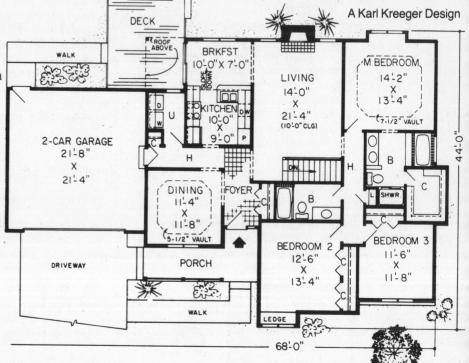

A Karl Kreeger Design

Your Privacy is Assured with Separate Bedroom Wing

No. 20114

Sturdy brick construction and arched window trim distinguish the facade of this efficient, one-level home. The central foyer boasts access to every area of the house: a wide-open kitchen with an adjoining breakfast room, a private bedroom wing, and a spacious, L-shaped living and dining room arrangement, where soaring ceilings are accentuated by the towering chimney of a cozy fireplace. Notice the convenient touches throughout the house: the handy garage entry to the breakfast room, the step-saving laundry located near the bedrooms, and double vanitied bath in the rear-facing master suite. Doors link both the breakfast and living rooms with an angular outdoor deck.

Main living area — 1,652 sq. ft.
Basement — 1,652 sq. ft.
Garage — 484 sq. ft.

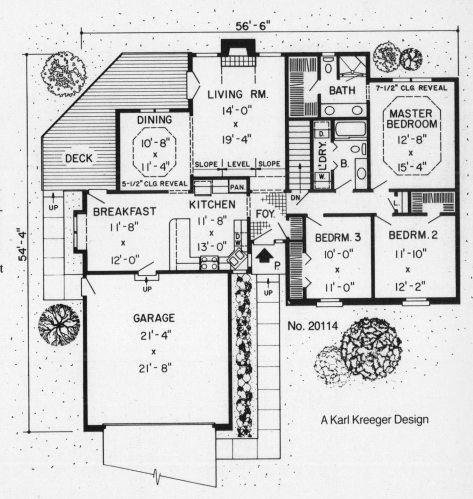

No. 20114

A Karl Kreeger Design

Capture the View

No. 20181

It's hard to equal the spacious outdoor feeling that abounds in this charming cedar and fieldstone gem. Abundant windows, decorative high ceilings, and wide-open active areas give this three-bedroom home its special character. You'll love all the conveniences built-in: a corner china cabinet in the formal dining room, a range-top island that divides the kitchen and breakfast room, and the handy utility area that includes a walk-in pantry, laundry room, powder room and handy garage access. To the left off the foyer, you'll find a full double-vanitied bath flanked by two large bedrooms. The master suite enjoys its own private luxury bath, plus a room-size walk-in closet.

Basement — 2,343 sq. ft.
Garage — 571 sq. ft.

Total living area — 2,360 sq. ft.

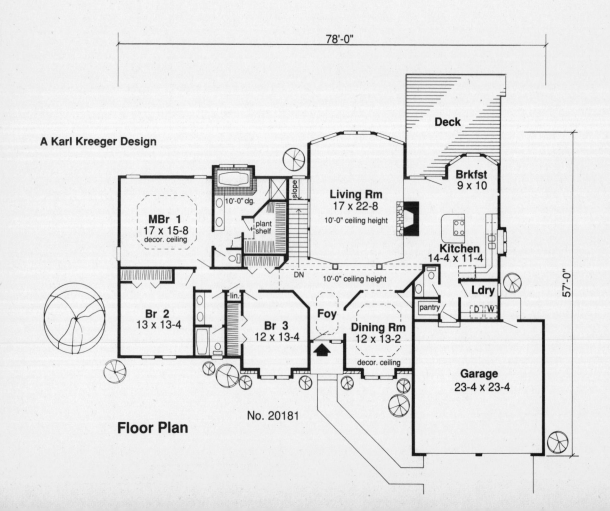

A Karl Kreeger Design

Floor Plan   No. 20181

Carefree Convenience

No. 20402

Although this adaptable, one-level gem features handicapped accessibility, it's an excellent choice for anyone looking for an easy-care home. Notice the extra-wide hallways, the master bath with roll-in shower, and specially designed kitchen with roll-out pantry and counters designed for wheelchair access. A sunny, spacious atmosphere envelopes each room, thanks to generous windows and sloping ceilings. Reach the deck from the U-shaped kitchen overlooking the fireplaced family room, and from the master suite. The dining room and living room, separated by a handy bar and just steps away from the kitchen, are ideal for entertaining. A hall bath serves the front bedrooms. This plan is built on a crawlspace foundation.

Garage — 617 sq. ft.
Porch — 210 sq. ft.

Total living area — 2,153 sq. ft.

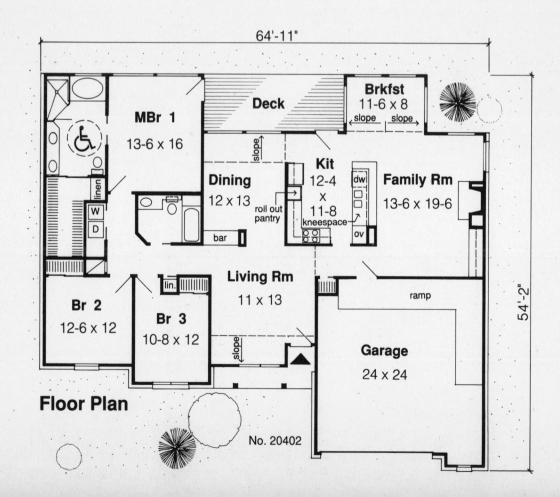

64'-11"

54'-2"

MBr 1 13-6 x 16

linen

W D

Deck

Brkfst 11-6 x 8

slope slope

Dining 12 x 13

roll out pantry

bar

Kit 12-4 x 11-8

kneespace

dw

ov

Family Rm 13-6 x 19-6

Living Rm 11 x 13

ramp

Br 2 12-6 x 12

Br 3 10-8 x 12

lin.

slope

Garage 24 x 24

slope

Floor Plan

No. 20402

Build This One-Level Home on a Budget

No. 90235

Here's an L-shaped ranch that will house your family in style without breaking your building budget. Stand in the central entry and enjoy the view of the large living room, a massive fireplace and the rear terrace beyond the sliding glass doors. Eat in the rear-facing privacy of the formal dining room, or in the spacious country kitchen. You'll appreciate the nearby garage entry when your arms are full of groceries. Three bedrooms and two full baths off the entry include the master suite with private terrace access.

**Main living area — 1,267 sq. ft.
Garage — 2-car**

No. 90235

Carefree
Convenience

No. 10674

One-level living is a breeze in this attractive, three bedroom beauty designed with your budget in mind. The covered porch adds a romantic touch to the clapboard facade. Step through the front door into a huge living room. Active areas surrounding a spacious patio at the rear of the house are served by a centrally-located galley kitchen. Eat in the formal dining room, or the handy breakfast room that adjoins the huge family room. A short hall leads to a handy full bath and two bedrooms. The master suite, tucked off the living room, features double closets and vanities for early-morning convenience. This plan is built on a slab foundation.

Garage — 465 sq. ft.

Total living area — 1,600 sq. ft.

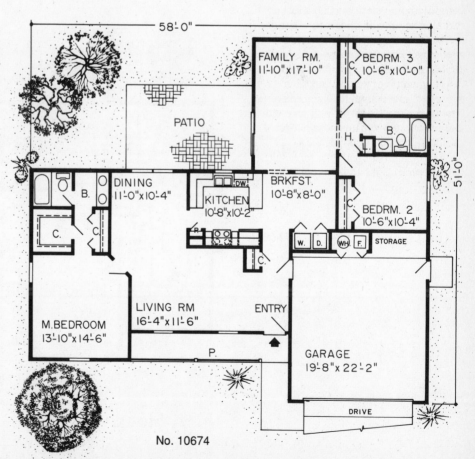

58'-0"

FAMILY RM.
11'-10"x17'-10"

BEDRM. 3
10'-6"x10'-0"

PATIO

H.

B.

DINING
11'-0"x10'-4"

BRKFST.
10'-8"x8'-0"

51'-0"

B.

KITCHEN
10'-8"x10'-2"

dw.

C.

BEDRM. 2
10'-6"x10'-4"

C.

C.

W. D. WH. F. STORAGE

M.BEDROOM
13'-10"x14'-6"

LIVING RM.
16'-4"x11'-6"

ENTRY

GARAGE
19'-8"x22'-2"

P.

DRIVE

No. 10674

Have It All

No. 20139

Three bedrooms, two baths, and an attached garage on one level; what more could you ask for? How about a classic brick and clapboard exterior adorned with an old-fashioned bay window? Or an elegant, fireplaced living room that flows into a formal dining room with sliders to a rear deck? This unique ranch also features a compact kitchen that opens to the dining room for a spacious feeling. The location of the well-appointed master suite behind the garage insures your privacy, and will spoil you with its double-vanitied bath and room-sized closet. Be sure to notice the skylit charm of the full bath that serves the bedrooms off the living room hall.

Basement — 1,488 sq. ft.
Garage — 484 sq. ft.

Total living area — 1,488 sq. ft.

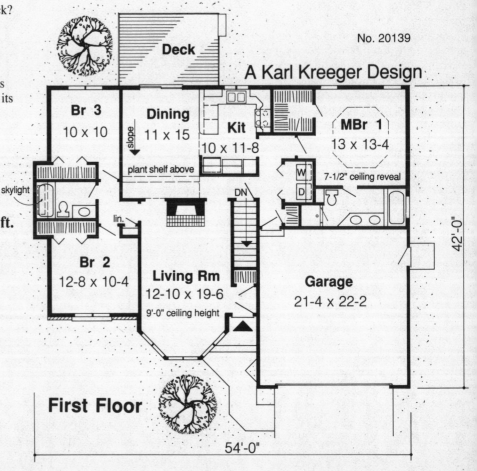

No. 20139

A Karl Kreeger Design

Deck

Br 3
10 x 10

Dining
11 x 15

Kit
10 x 11-8

MBr 1
13 x 13-4

7-1/2" ceiling reveal

slope

plant shelf above

skylight

lin.

DN

Br 2
12-8 x 10-4

Living Rm
12-10 x 19-6

9'-0" ceiling height

Garage
21-4 x 22-2

W
D

42'-0"

54'-0"

First Floor

Gardener's Dream House

No. 20086

Start planning the landscaping. The shape of this delightful one-level home offers unlimited opportunities for a charming entry garden. And, with extra-large windows and a massive deck, you can enjoy every part of your yard in any season. This convenient plan unites living and dining rooms at the rear of the house. For family meals, the island kitchen features a cozy nook with easy access to the deck. Bedrooms, isolated in their own wing for maximum quiet, include a spacious master suite with skylit bath.

Basement — 1,628 sq. ft.

Garage — 434 sq. ft.

Total living area — 1,628 sq. ft.

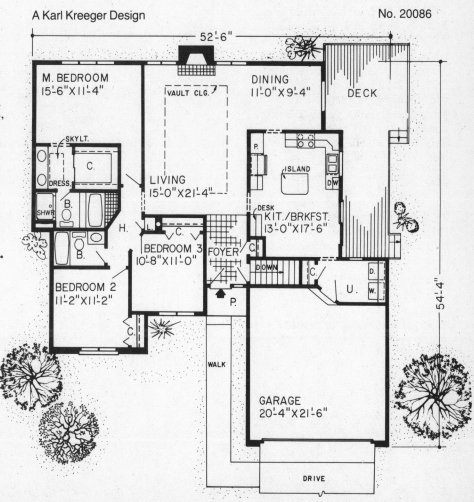

A Karl Kreeger Design   No. 20086

52'-6"

M. BEDROOM
15'-6"X11'-4"

VAULT CLG.

DINING
11'-0"X9'-4"

DECK

SKYLT.

C.

LIVING
15'-0"X21'-4"

DRESS.

B.

SHWR

P.

ISLAND

DW

DESK

KIT./BRKFST.
13'-0"X17'-6"

H.

L.

C.

C.

FOYER

B.

BEDROOM 3
10'-8"X11'-0"

DOWN

C.

D.

U.

W.

BEDROOM 2
11'-2"X11'-2"

C.

P.

54'-4"

WALK

GARAGE
20'-4"X21'-6"

DRIVE

Carefree and Cozy

No. 91618

The multiple peaks of this one-level home hint at the intriguing plan you'll find inside. The central foyer opens to a many-sided great hall, which offers access to every area of the house. To the left, the fireplaced living room with coved ceilings and massive front window flows into a formal dining room with built-in corner cabinet. Step back to the island kitchen that adjoins a sunny breakfast bay and comfortable family room overlooking the deck. You'll find three bedrooms tucked behind the garage, off a hallway that leads past the den, powder room, full bath, and utility room with garage access. The master suite at the rear of the house is a special treat, with its bay window, coved ceilings, and private bath with double vanities and garden spa. This plan is built on a crawlspace foundation.

Garage — 2-car

Total living area — 2,087 sq. ft.

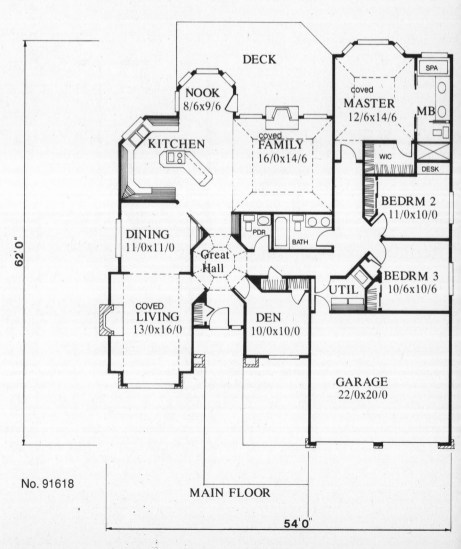

No. 91618

MAIN FLOOR

Garden Courtyard Protects Privacy

No. 90547

Attention to detail and concern for privacy set this one-level masterpiece apart from the standard ranch home. The tiled entry is flanked by a curving, sunken living room and a private dining room overlooking the back yard. Walk past formal areas, so perfect for entertaining, to a sun-filled family area that includes an efficient, U-shaped kitchen, an angular breakfast bay with back yard access, and a fireplaced family room with a built-in bar. Two rear bedrooms share a full bath. But, the master suite at the front of the house, with its raised garden tub overlooking a private courtyard, double vanities, and walk-in wardrobe, is reason alone to choose this luxurious home.

Main living area — 2,178 sq. ft.
Garage — 2-car

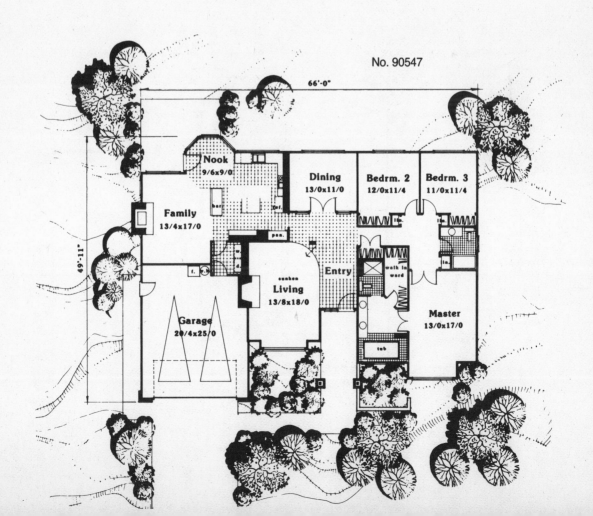

No. 90547

Solar Help for your Budget

No. 91010

From outside, you'd never know this was a one-level home. Soaring roof lines and clerestory windows give this three-bedroom contemporary a wonderful feeling of height. Inside the central entry, the drama continues. Enjoy a panoramic view of the sunken living room, dining room, sunroom and backyard beyond. Walk down the hall to the bedroom wing, isolated for quiet hours away from living areas. On a sunny day, open the sunroom doors in the family room. At night, the massive fireplace will keep you warm. You won't have to use the furnace at all. This plan is built on a combination slab and crawlspace foundation.

Garage — 2-car

Total living area — 1,796

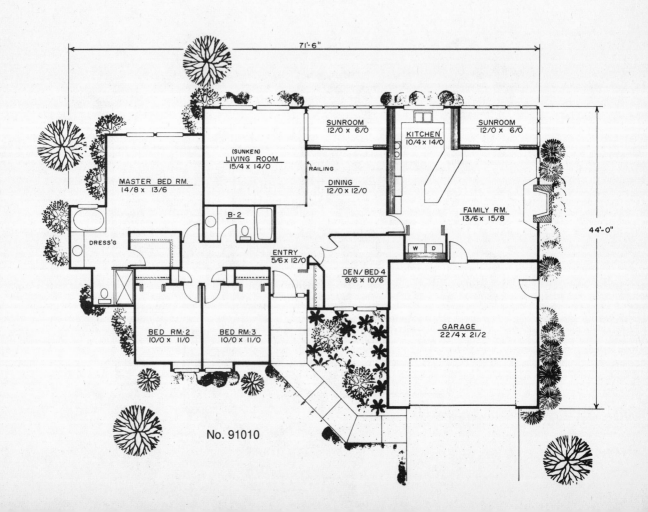

No. 91010

Sunny Charm

No. 20407

If you enjoy carefree convenience and a cheerful atmosphere, this brick and stucco suncatcher will be hard to resist. Wide open space characterizes the active areas of this three-bedroom charmer, beginning with the skylit, columned foyer that divides the dining room from the study. Walk two ways from the quiet study space: into the soaring elegance of the rear facing master suite, or the two front bedrooms that share an adjoining full bath with double vanities. The fireplaced living room, with its handy wet bar and shelf-lined walls, opens to a large rear deck. To the left, you'll find a sunny breakfast room and family room surrounding the large, well-equipped kitchen.

Main living area — 2,753 sq. ft.
Garage — sq. ft.

Total living area — 2,753 sq. ft.

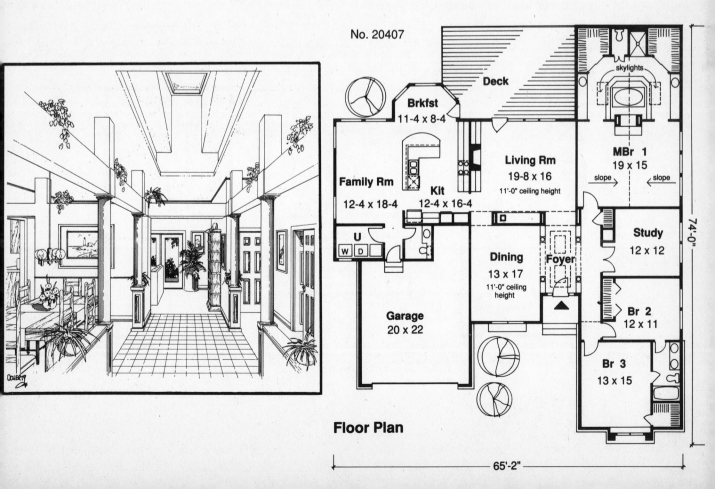

No. 20407

Floor Plan

Walled Flower Court Adorns Attractive Facade

No. 90227

A two-way fireplace, a wide-open plan, and generous windows give this one-level home a cozy ambiance you'll treasure for years. The entry hall leads three ways: into the private wing that houses four bedrooms and two full baths, to the formal living and dining rooms so perfect for entertaining, and back to family areas at the rear of the house. Be sure to notice the special privacy of the rear master suite with sliders to its own terrace. Imagine yourself in the gourmet kitchen, complete with barbecue and pass-through convenience to both the breakfast nook and rustic family room. There's even a workshop off the garage for the hobbyist of the house.

Living area — 2,646 sq. ft.
Garage — 2-car

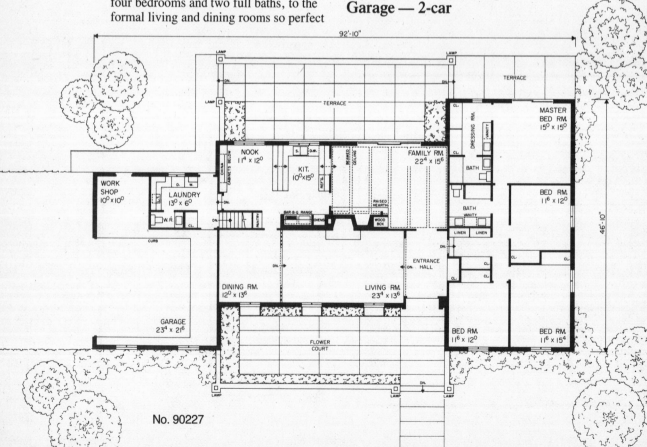

No. 90227

Dramatic Impressions

No. 20451

Picture yourself relaxing in the dappled sunlight of the partially covered deck that spans the rear of this unusual, sprawling home. Entertaining will be easy in this spectacular setting, whether you choose the large, soaring living room off the vaulted skylit foyer or the cozy family room that shares the backyard view with the glass-walled breakfast room it adjoins. The kitchen easily serves every area, including the elegant formal dining room at the front of the house. Two bedrooms, tucked in a quiet spot off the family room, flank a full bath with double vanities. The master suite, tucked off behind the garage, features private deck access and a magnificent bath with a garden tub surrounded by glass block walls.

Basement — 2,084 sq. ft.

Garage — 2-car

Total living area — 2,084 sq. ft.

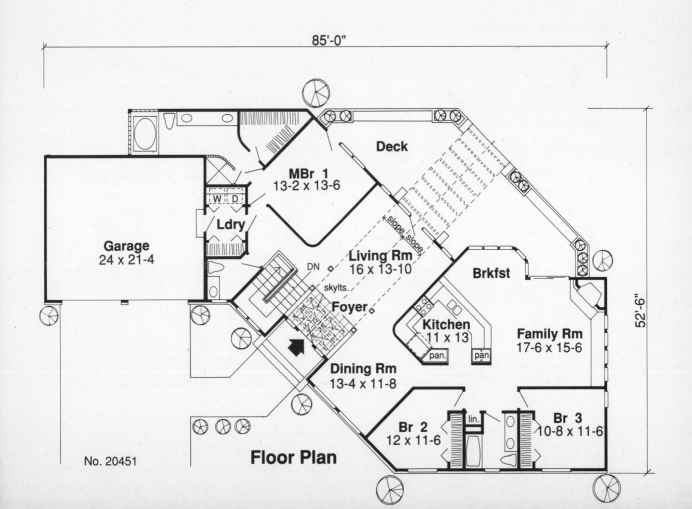

Floor Plan

No. 20451

Fireplace Dominates Rustic Design

No. 90409

The ample porch of this charming home deserves a rocking chair, and there's room for two or three if you'd like. The front entry opens to an expansive great room with a soaring cathedral ceiling. Flanked by the master suite and two bedrooms with a full bath, the great room is separated from formal dining by a massive fireplace. The convenient galley kitchen adjoins a sunny breakfast nook, perfect for informal family dining.

Living area — 1,670 sq. ft.

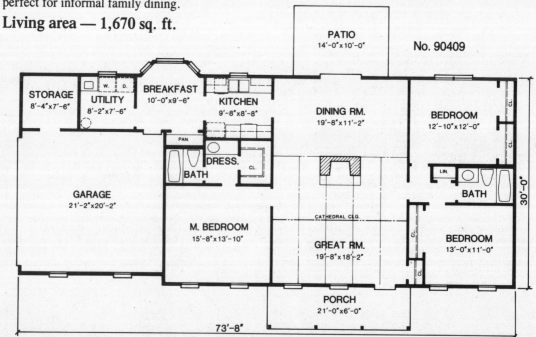

Foyer Isolates Bedroom Wing

No. 20087

Don't worry about waking up the kids. They'll sleep soundly in a quiet atmosphere away from main living areas, on a hallway off the foyer of this charming one-level. Sunny and open, the living room features a window-wall flanking a massive fireplace, and access to a deck at the rear of the house. The adjoining dining room boasts recessed ceilings, and pass-through convenience to the kitchen and breakfast room. You'll find the master suite, tucked behind the two-car garage for maximum quiet, a pleasant retreat that includes double vanities, a walk-in closet, and both shower and tub.

First floor — 1,568 sq. ft.
Bsement — 1,568 sq. ft.
Garage — 484 sq. ft.

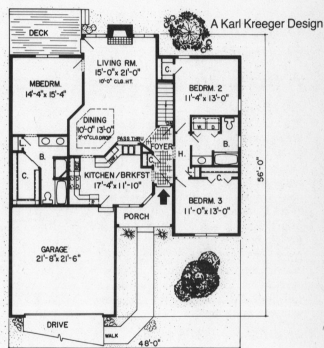

A Karl Kreeger Design

Glass-walled Family Room Invites Entertaining

No. 10466

With convenient access through the breakfast nook, a well-stocked wetbar opens into both the living room and the family room. The beamed ceiling of the living room plus its hearth-rimmed fireplace will appeal to family and guests alike. The kitchen sink is bathed in light from the corner greenhouse windows and flanked by plenty of cabinet and counter space. The four bedrooms of this well-organized plan are located along one wall of the home. The master suite features a corner window-seat and a dressing room with its own skylight.

First floor — 2,285 sq. ft.
Garage — 483 sq. ft.

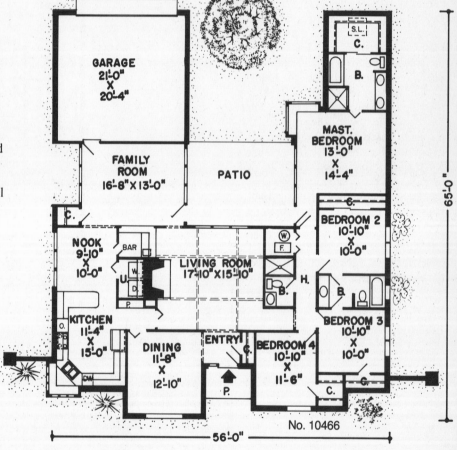

Private and Practical

No. 91417

Streetside windows and a covered entry present an inviting facade to guests who enter this easy-care contemporary. Lead them into the sunny living room right off the entry, which opens to a formal dining room for elegant suppers. Walk straight back to informal areas, which include a vaulted family room crowned by a fireplace, and a bayed breakfast room and kitchen combination with island snack bar. To reach the quiet bedroom wing tucked behind the garage, just walk past the study. You'll find a luxurious master suite with private deck entry, his-and-hers walk-in closets, and a full bath complete with glass block-enclosed shower for busy mornings. Another full bath serves the second bedroom.

Main living area — 2,282 sq. ft.
Garage — 2-car

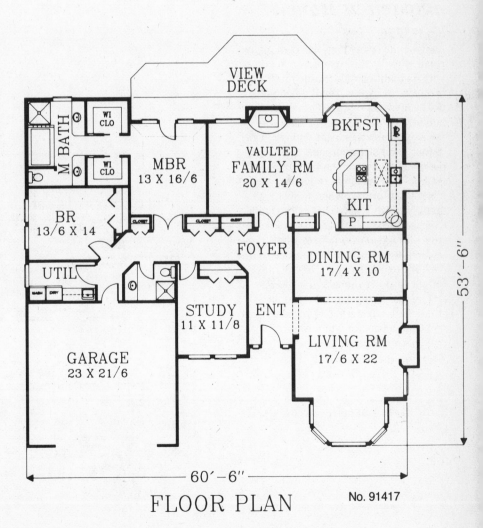

FLOOR PLAN   No. 91417

Spanish Infuence in a Spacious Ranch

No. 99226

Imagine the sunny days and cool nights you'll enjoy in this Spanish-style home, with its traditional fluted tile roofing, open air courtyards, small reflecting pool, and sprawling tiled terraces. The interior layout offers a fine blend of family and entertainment settings. Up to four good-size bedrooms are possible, all grouped on the left end of the house. The family room provides a pleasant, informal gathering spot, highlighted by a cathedral ceiling with exposed wood beams and a snackbar pass-through to the kitchen. The kitchen itself is a wonderful place to cook for two or twenty, Hold parties or formal sit-down dinners in the long, rectangular living and dining room combination, featuring a fireplace focal point and a band of windows overlooking the courtyard

Basement — 2,261 sq. ft.

Garage — 3-car

Total living area — 2,261 sq. ft.

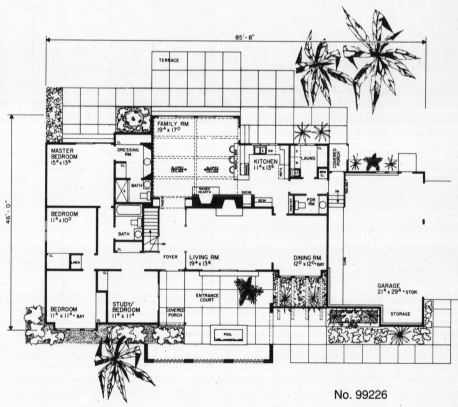

No. 99226

172

A Roomy Ranch with Superior Style

No. 99237

The real highlight of this comfortable three-bedroom home is its magnificent family room. Here's nearly 300 square feet of entertaining and recreation space, with a raised hearth fireplace for cozier gatherings. The exposed wood beam ceiling is a traditional touch carried through in the adjoining kitchen. Put a butcher block work table in the center of the roomy kitchen as the perfect complement to a well-planned work area. The sunken living room has a finesse all its own, with a second fireplace and step-up to formal dining. Sleeping quarters are allocated their fair share of convenience and comfort, including two full baths and ample closet space. This plan is built on a slab with an optional combination basement-crawlspace foundation. Please specify when ordering

Basement — 2,029 sq. ft.
Garage — two-car

Total living area — 2,029 sq. ft.

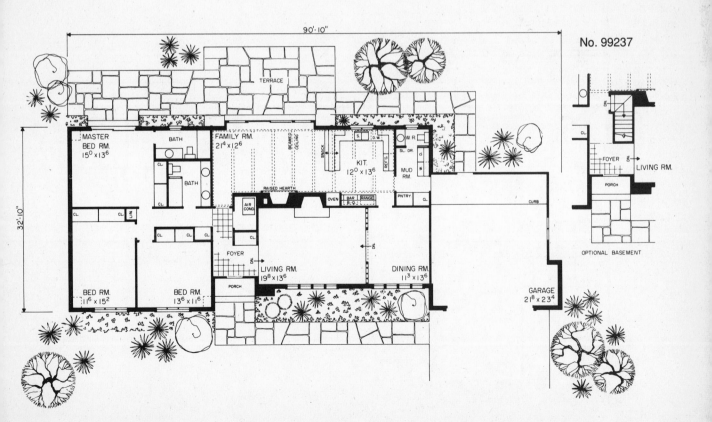

No. 99237

Woodside Ranch

No. 99219

This cost-conscious ranch is a great option for the first-time home buyer - without having to sacrifice space for economy. A wooded site would be ideal in making the most of the country cottage look of the exterior. Inside you'll enjoy the ease of one-floor living. Depending on your family's needs, you'll have either three bedrooms or two bedrooms with a separate tv-study room. The kitchen offers a four-seat snack counter and pass-through to the breakfast room. and ample space for a handy deck in its own alcove. The cathedral ceiling in the combined living-dining area creates a sense of spaciousness, while the center fireplace with raised hearth adds that touch of homey comfort.

Daylighting has been successfully achieved with a substantial number of windows as well as skylights in the covered porch to bring more light into the living areas. Two full baths, a two-car garage, and room for a workshop are included in this home.

Basement — 1,547 sq. ft.
Garage — 2-car

Total living area — 1,547 sq. ft.

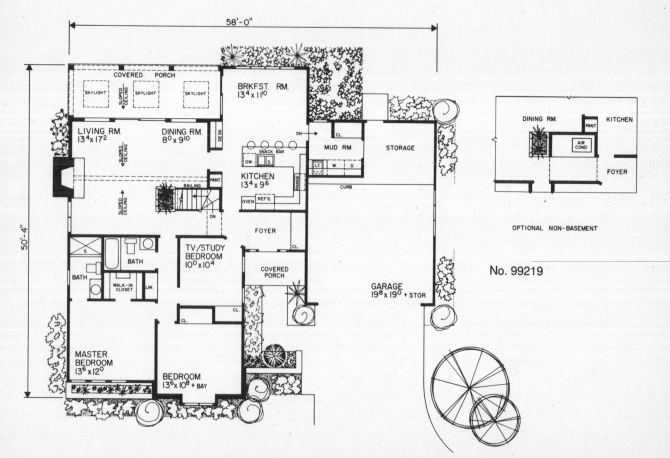

Tudor Sun Catcher

No. 90249

Face the rear of this efficient ranch home south to take advantage of the sun's free energy. The breakfast room, and the soaring living and dining rooms feature rear-facing glass walls, providing a sunny atmosphere enhanced by the warmth of a massive fireplace. The attached covered porch, accessible to both living and breakfast rooms, adds to the outdoor ambiance. The centrally located kitchen features a handy snack bar and built-in pantry and planning desk, just steps away from the storage area off the attached garage. You'll love the cheerful atmosphere in the three front-facing bedrooms, which share a private corner of the house with two full baths.

Main living area — 1,584 sq. ft.
Garage — 2-car

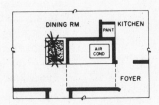

OPTIONAL NON-BASEMENT

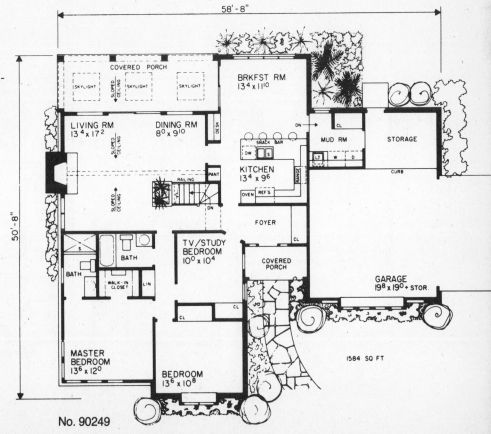

No. 90249

Living Areas Warmed by Massive Fireplace

No. 10752

Here's a handsome home for the family that enjoys one-level living. Skylights, sloping ceilings, and an absence of walls give active areas an irresistable, spacious atmosphere. And, with a floor-to-ceiling window wall in the living room and French doors in the dining room, interior spaces enjoy a pleasing unity with the great outdoors. Whether you're in the mood for formal or informal dining, the centrally located kitchen will make mealtime a breeze. Three bedrooms, each featuring a walk-in closet, occupy their own quiet wing off the foyer. The front bedrooms share a full bath with double vanities. The master suite at the rear of the house enjoys a private bath.

First floor — 1,705 sq. ft.
Garage — 488 sq. ft.

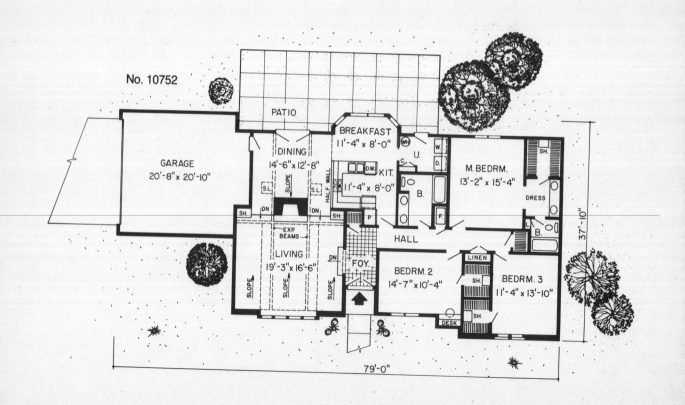

Ranch Offers Attractive Windows

No. 10569

This four bedroom ranch offers two full baths with plenty of closet space. Also in this design, the living room has a sloping, open beamed ceiling with a fireplace and built-in fireplace bookshelves. The dining room is connected to the foyer and has a vaulted ceiling, adding to an already spacious room. The kitchen has an ample amount of dining space available and has sliding glass doors that lead out onto a brick patio. A half-bath with shower is located next to the kitchen as well as a pantry and washer/dryer space for more convenience. A two car garage is available in this plan.

First floor — 1,840 sq. ft.
Basement — 1,803 sq. ft.
Garage — 445 sq. ft.

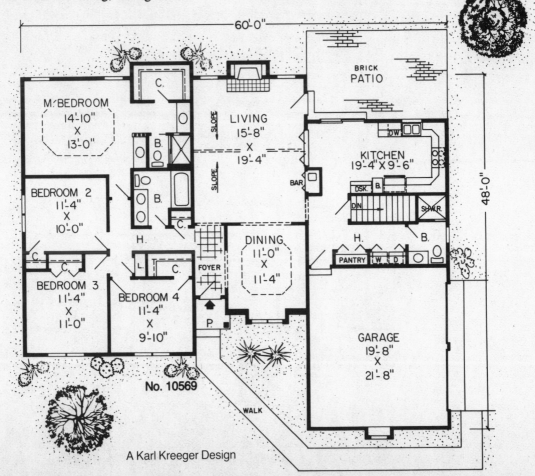

No. 10569

A Karl Kreeger Design

Carefree Contemporary

No. 90697

This carefree ranch combines vertical siding with rows of tall windows for a contemporary flavor. A covered porch opens to the central foyer, flanked by the formal living and dining rooms. A corner fireplace adds intrigue to the elegant, sunny living room. You'll find another fireplace in the skylit family room at the rear of the house, where a greenhouse bay, overlooking the terrace, adds an outdoor feeling. Even the adjoining kitchen benefits from this cheerful, sun-washed atmosphere. A hallway to the right leads to the quiet area of the house. The two front bedrooms are served by the double-vanitied hall bath. The master suite boasts a private bath, a backyard view, and loads of closet space.

Basement — 1,597 sq. ft.

Garage — 2-car

Total living area — 1,597 sq. ft.

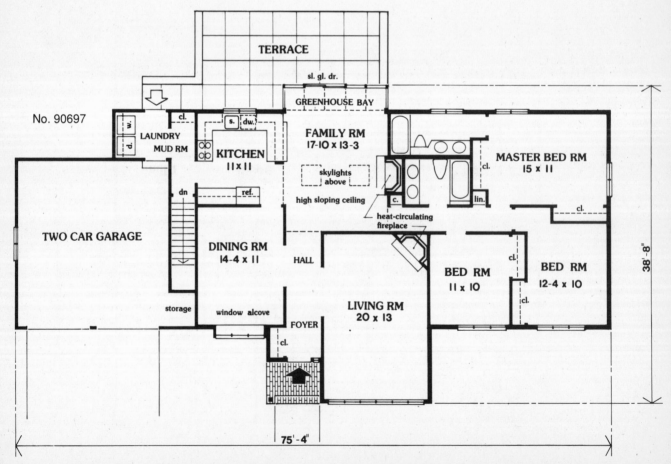

Ranch with Handicapped Access

No. 20403

This comfortable Ranch has the convenience of an open floor plan as well as handicapped access from the front door, garage and deck. Life centers in the area surrounding the galley kitchen. The family room has a large hearth and fireplace, and opens onto an extensive deck off the rear of the house. The space-saving kitchen serves both a formal dining room and a sunny, bow-windowed breakfast room. Cathedral ceilings in the master bedroom set off a wall of windows. A walk-in closet and a bath designed for handicapped use are also included. The other two bedrooms share a full bath. This plan is built on a crawlspace foundation.

Porch — 118 sq. ft.
Deck — 354 sq. ft.
Garage — 606 sq. ft.

Total living area — 1,734 sq. ft.

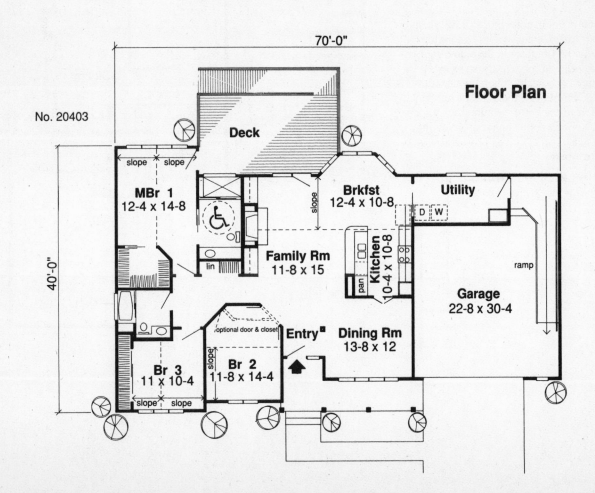

No. 20403

Floor Plan

70'-0"

40'-0"

Deck

MBr 1
12-4 x 14-8

Br 3
11 x 10-4

slope   slope

optional door & closet

slope

Br 2
11-8 x 14-4

lin

Family Rm
11-8 x 15

Brkfst
12-4 x 10-8

slope

Kitchen
10-4 x 10-8

pan

Utility

D W

Garage
22-8 x 30-4

ramp

Entry

Dining Rm
13-8 x 12

slope   slope

A Perfect Union of Inside and Out

No. 90382

Here's one-level living with a contemporary twist. Stepping through the entry of this exciting home, you can see right into the back yard through sliders in the vaulted, sunken living room. And, the sunlight, pouring through clerestory windows above and the glass wall at the rear, adds a wide-open feeling to this dynamic room. Imagine cozy family gatherings around the fireplace in the adjoining family and dining rooms, just steps away from the efficient kitchen for easy mealtimes. Bedrooms, tucked off a hallway to the left of the entry, feature floor-to-ceiling windows for a sunny, open feeling. The master suite enjoys private access to the rear patio.

Living area — 1,421 sq. ft.
Garage — 2-car

No. 90382

Floor Plan

Surrounded with Sunshine

No. 20092

Here's a cheerful one-level, characterized by lots of oversized windows and an airy plan. Garage and front entries open to the central foyer, which leads right into a huge, fireplaced living room and a view of the back yard. Bask in the sun as you sip your morning coffee in the skylit dining room with sliders to the deck. And, look at that adjoining, U-shaped kitchen. You can't ask for a more convenient arrangement! Down a short hall off the living room, three bedrooms share a corner of the house away from active areas. Notice the walk-in closets in the master suite and front bedroom, the skylit second bath, and the luxurious master bath with its vaulted ceilings, double vanities and raised tub.

Main living area — 1,693 sq. ft.
Basement — 1,693 sq. ft.
Garage — 484 sq. ft.

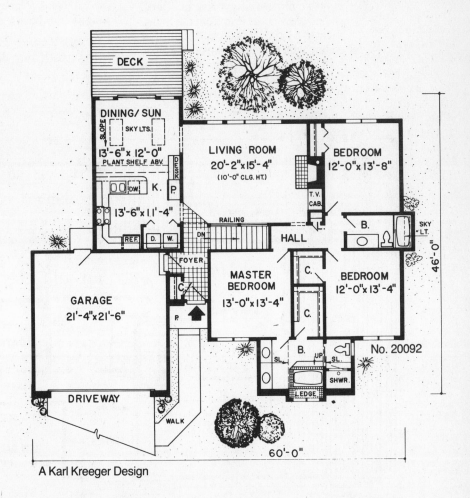

A Karl Kreeger Design

All Year Leisure

No. 90630

Natural materials used inside and out, and good design, make this ranch house easy to build and easy to live in. Three sliding glass doors lead from the living room to a large glass deck. A cathedral ceiling with exposed beams and a stone wall with heat-circulating fireplace give the interior a charming and solid look. A table for informal meals separates the far end of the living room from the kitchen which opens either into the hall or the handy laundry-storage mud-room inside the back door. Two good sized double bedrooms, a single bedroom, and two full baths complete the bedroom wing. In this house, simplicity is the key.

Living Area — 1,207 sq. ft. (plus mudroom-laundry and deck)

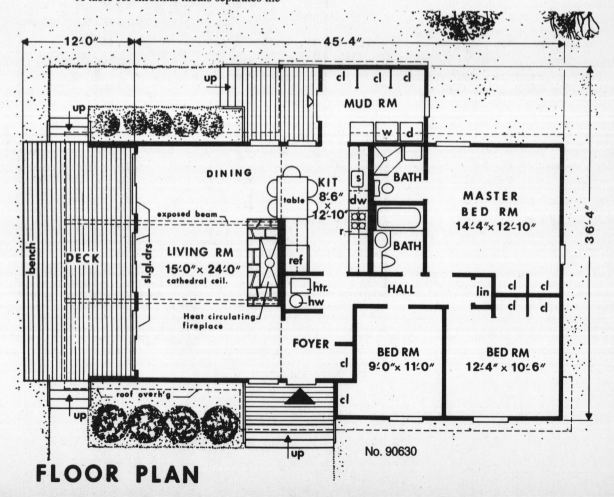

FLOOR PLAN

Built-Ins Add Extra Storage Space

No. 90207

This versatile, one-level plan keeps active and quiet areas separate for maximum privacy. A massive fireplace with raised hearth divides the central entry from the huge gathering room. Notice how common areas flow together. Three sliding doors off the gathering and dining rooms and the glass walls of the bayed breakfast nook combine with this open arrangement to create a spacious feeling throughout the area. Need warm weather living space? Retreat to the surrounding rear terrace for stargazing or a candlelit dinner. A hallway tucked off the entry leads to three bedrooms and two full baths. You'll appreciate the generous closet space and the private terrace access in the master suite.

**Living area — 1,366 sq. ft.
Garage — 2-car**

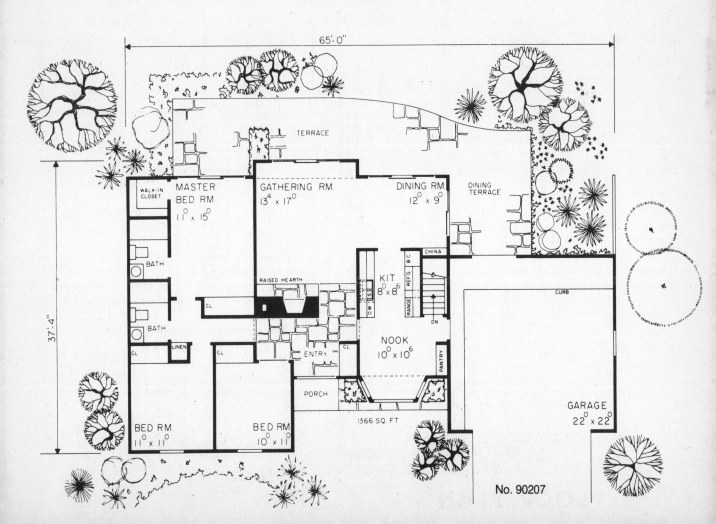

No. 90207

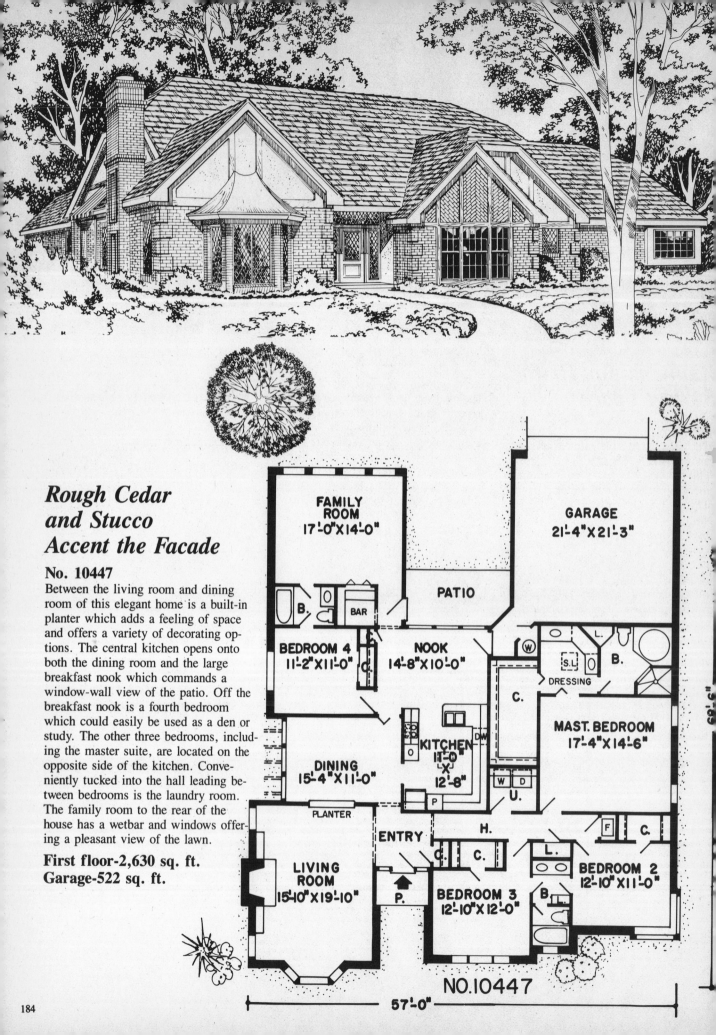

Rough Cedar and Stucco Accent the Facade

No. 10447

Between the living room and dining room of this elegant home is a built-in planter which adds a feeling of space and offers a variety of decorating options. The central kitchen opens onto both the dining room and the large breakfast nook which commands a window-wall view of the patio. Off the breakfast nook is a fourth bedroom which could easily be used as a den or study. The other three bedrooms, including the master suite, are located on the opposite side of the kitchen. Conveniently tucked into the hall leading between bedrooms is the laundry room. The family room to the rear of the house has a wetbar and windows offering a pleasant view of the lawn.

**First floor-2,630 sq. ft.
Garage-522 sq. ft.**

FAMILY ROOM 17'-0" X 14'-0"

GARAGE 21'-4" X 21'-3"

PATIO

B.

BAR

BEDROOM 4 11'-2" X 11'-0"

NOOK 14'-8" X 10'-0"

W

C.

S.U.

DRESSING

B.

C.

MAST. BEDROOM 17'-4" X 14'-6"

KITCHEN 11'-0" X 12'-8"

DINING 15'-4" X 11'-0"

W   D

U.

P

H.

L.

F   C.

PLANTER

ENTRY

C.   C.

BEDROOM 2 12'-10" X 11'-0"

LIVING ROOM 15'-10" X 19'-10"

P.

BEDROOM 3 12'-10" X 12'-0"

B.

NO. 10447

57'-0"

69'-6"

Family Plan

No. 90573

Here's one-level living on a grand scale. The central entry offers entering guests an immediate view of a spectacular fire-placed living and dining room arrangement separated by a single, curving step. The master suite, with its towering stacked window and garden tub enclosed by a fence for privacy, is just around the corner. A short hall past the den leads two ways: to the bedrooms and full bath tucked behind the garage, and to the informal areas overlooking the backyard. You'll appreciate the wide-open atmosphere that large, abundant windows, sliding glass doors, and an open plan bring this area. From the fireplaced family room to the island kitchen and sunny nook, this is a spot designed for family interaction.

Main living area — 2,417 sq. ft.
Garage — 3-car

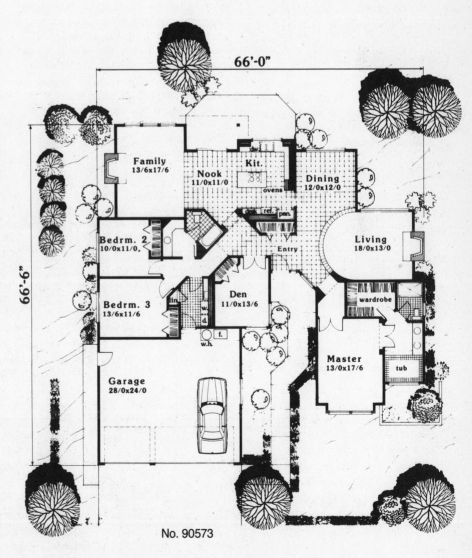

No. 90573

Affordable Energy-Saver Loaded with Amenities

No. 90680

This attractive ranch, which possesses many features only available in larger homes, is the perfect choice for the budget-conscious family looking for a touch of luxury. Look at the wide-open arrangement of the living and dining rooms, bathed in light from skylights overhead and large expanses of front and rear-facing glass. A heat circulating fireplace helps lower your energy bills. Enjoy your morning coffee in the greenhouse setting of the dinette bay off the kitchen. Or, on a summer morning, the terrace off the dining room is a nice place to spread out with the Sunday paper. In the bedroom wing off the foyer lie three bedrooms, served by two full baths. Look at the private deck complete with hot tub off the master suite.

Living area — 1,393 sq. ft.
Basement — 1,393 sq. ft.
Garage-laundry — 542 sq. ft.
Front porch — 195 sq. ft.

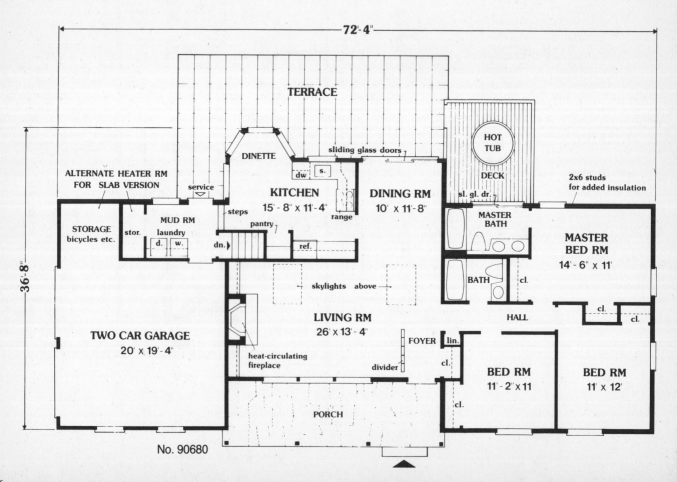

No. 90680

Compact Plan Features Private Patio

No. 10772

A walled garden, diagonal wood accents, and rough-hewn timber add loads of curbside appeal to this one-level home designed for a narrow lot. Inside, there's a lot of living space packed into this compact plan. An efficient galley kitchen links formal and informal dining rooms for easy meal service. Decorative columns and a single step separate the dining room from the fireplaced living room without confining walls. And, double sliding glass doors to the patio add to the outdoor feeling in this spacious room. Two bedrooms include the master suite, where you'll find sliders to a private corner of the patio, double closets, and a full bath.

Main living area — 1,280 sq. ft.
Garage — one-car

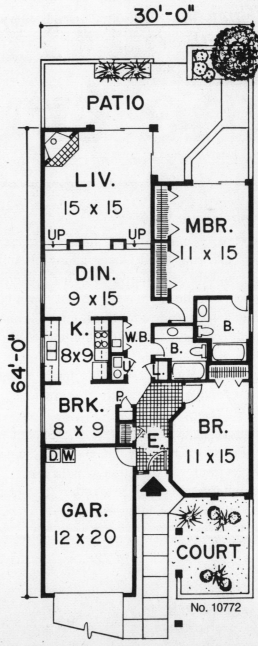

No. 10772

Everything you need to make your dream come true!

You pay only a fraction of the original cost for home designs by respected professionals.

You've picked your dream home!

You can already see it standing on your lot... you can see yourselves in your new home... enjoying family, entertaining guests, celebrating holidays. All that remains ahead are the details. That's where we can help.

Whether you plan to build-it-yourself, be your own contractor, or hand your plans over to an outside contractor, your Garlinghouse blueprints provide the perfect beginning for putting yourself in your dream home right away.

We even make it simple for you to make professional design modifications. We can also provide a materials list for greater economy.

My grandfather, L.F. Garlinghouse, started a tradition of quality when he founded this company in 1907. For over 80 years, homeowners and builders have relied on us for accurate, complete, professional blueprints. Our plans help you get results fast... and save money, too! These pages will give you all the information you need to order. So get started now... I know you'll love your new Garlinghouse home!

Sincerely,

Here's What You Get!

1 *Exterior Elevations*

Exact scale views of the front, rear, and both sides of your home, showing exterior materials, details, and all necessary measurements.

2 *Detailed Floor Plans*

Showing the placement of all interior walls, the dimensions of rooms, doors, windows, stairways, and other details.

3 *Foundation Plan*

With footings and all load-bearing points as applicable to your home, including all necessary notations and dimensions.

The foundation style supplied varies from home to home. Local conditions and practices will determine whether a basement, crawl-space, or a slab is best for you. Your professional contractor can easily make the necessary adaption.

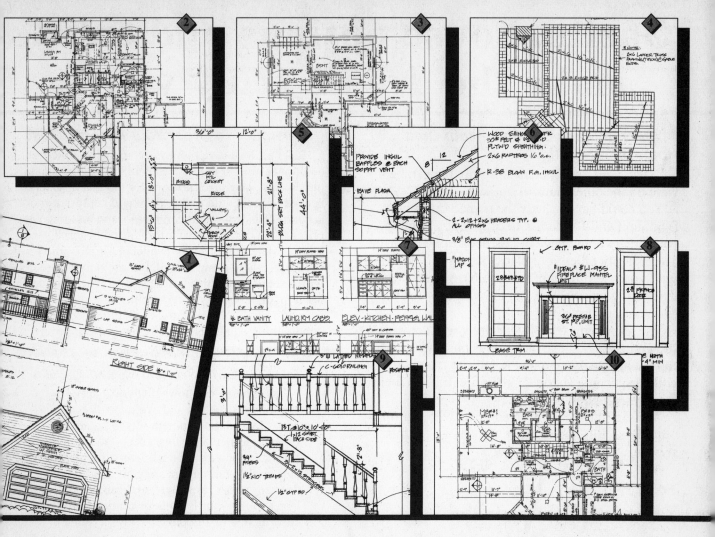

◆ Roof Plan

All information necessary to construct the roof for your home is included. Many blueprints contain framing plans showing all of the roof elements, so you'll know how these details look and fit together.

◆ Universal Plot Plan

The view of your home from above, with hypothetical lot outlines, all ready for your lot dimensions, property-line setbacks and site improvement specifications.

◆ Typical Wall Sections

Detailed views of your home, as though sliced from top to bottom. These drawings clarify exterior and interior wall construction, insulation, flooring, and roofing details.

Depending on your specific geography and climate, your home will be built with either 2x4 or 2x6 exterior walls. Most professional contractors can easily adapt plans for either requirement.

◆ Kitchen & Bath Cabinet Details

These plans show the specific details and placement of the cabinets in your kitchen, bathroom, and utility room as applicable. They also show any other special interior features. Customizing these areas is simpler beginning with these details.

◆ Fireplace Details

When your home includes one or more fireplaces, these detailed drawings will help your mason with their construction and appearance. It is easy to review details with professionals when you have the plans for reference.

◆ Stair Details

If stairs are part of the design you selected, specific plans are included for their construction and details.

◆ Schematic Electrical Layouts

The suggested locations for all of your switches, outlets, and fixtures are indicated on these drawings. They are practical as they are, but they are also a solid taking-off point for any personal adaptions.

Also available, is a money-saving Materials List.

Plus...

FREE

Specifications and Contract Form

FREE

14-page Energy Conservation Guide.

TURN THE PAGE FOR THE EASY STEPS TO COMPLETE YOUR DREAM HOME ORDER!

Garlinghouse options and extras make the dream truly yours.

Reversed Plans Can Make Your Dream Home Just Right!

"That's our dream home... if only the garage were on the other side!"

You could have exactly the home you want by flipping it end-for-end. Check it out by holding your dream home page of this book up to a mirror. Then simply order your plans "reversed". We'll send you one full set of mirror-image plans (with the writing backwards) as a master guide for you and your builder.

The remaining sets of your order will come as shown in this book so the dimensions and specifications are easily read on the job site... but they will be specially stamped "REVERSED" so there is no construction confusion.

We can only send reversed plans with multiple-set orders. But, there is no extra charge for this service.

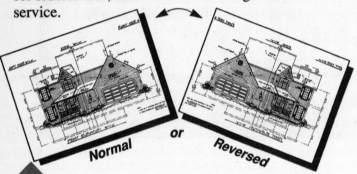

Normal or Reversed

Modifying Your Garlinghouse Home Plan

Easy modifications to your dream home... minor non-structural changes, simple materials substitutions... can be made between you and your builder.

However, if you are considering making major changes to your design, we strongly recommend that you use an architect or a professional designer. And, since you have already started with our complete detailed blueprints, the cost of those expensive professional services will be significantly less.

Our Reproducible Mylars Make Modifications Easier

They provide a design professional with the right way to make changes directly to your Garlinghouse home plans and then print as many copies of the modified plans as you need.

Prices range from $375-$525 plus shipping. Reproducible mylars aren't available for plan numbers 19000 through 19999, and 90000 and above.

Call 1-800-235-5700 to find out more.

Remember To Order Your Materials List

It'll help you save money. Available at a modest additional charge, the Materials List gives the quantity, dimensions, and specifications for the major materials needed to build your home. You will get faster, more accurate bids from your contractors and building suppliers — and avoid paying for unused materials and waste. Materials Lists are available for all home plans except as otherwise indicated, but can only be ordered with a set of home plans. Due to differences in local building codes, regional requirements, and homeowner/builder preferences... electrical, plumbing & heating/air conditioning equipment requirements aren't provided.

How Many Sets Of Plans Will You Need?

The Standard 8-Set Construction Package

Our experience shows that you'll speed every step of construction and avoid costly building errors by ordering enough sets to go around. Each tradesperson wants a set — the general contractor and all subcontractors; foundation, electrical, plumbing, heating/air conditioning, drywall, finish carpenters, and cabinet shop. Don't forget your lending institution, building deparment and, of course, a set for yourself.

The Minimum 5-Set Construction Package

If you're comfortable with arduous follow-up, this package can save you a few dollars. You might have enough copies to go around if work goes exactly as scheduled and no plans are lost or damaged. But for only $30 more, the 8-set package eliminates these worries.

The Single-Set Decision-Maker Package

We offer this set so you can study the blueprints to plan your dream home in detail. But remember... one set is never enough to build your home... and they're copyrighted.

Questions?

Call our customer service number at 1-203-632-0500.

An important note:

All plans are drawn to conform to one or more of the industry's major national building standards. However, due to the variety of local building regulations, your plan may need to be modified to comply with local requirements — snow loads, energy loads, seismic zones, etc. Do check them fully and consult your local building officials.

A few states require that all building plans used be drawn by an architect registered in that state. While having your plans reviewed and stamped by such an architect may be prudent, laws requiring non-conforming plans like ours to be completely redrawn forces you to unnecessarily pay very large fees. If your state has such a law, we strongly recommend you contact your state representative to protest.

Important Shipping Information

Your order is processed immediately. Allow 10 working days from our receipt of your order for normal UPS delivery. Save time with your credit card and our "800" number. UPS *must* have a street address or Rural Route Box number — never a post office box. Use a work address if no one is home during the day.

Orders being shipped to Alaska, Hawaii, APO, FPO or Post Ofice Boxes must go via First Class Mail. Please include the proper postage.

Canadian Orders and Shipping:

To our friends in Canada, we have a plan design affiliate in Kitchener, Ontario. This relationship will help you avoid the delays and charges associated with shipments from the United States. Morever, our affiliate is familiar with the building requirements in your community and country.

Please submit all Canadian plan orders to:

The Garlinghouse Company, Inc.
20 Cedar Street North
Kitchener, Ontario N2H, 2W8
(519) 743-4169

Blueprint Price Schedule (stated in U.S. dollars)	
Standard Constuction Package (8 sets)	$215.00
Minimum Construction Package (5 sets)	185.00
Single-Set Package	140.00
Each Additional Set (ordered w/one above)	20.00
Materials List (with plan order only)	20.00

We prefer payments in U.S. Currency. If you, however, are sending Canadian funds, please add 20% to the prices of the plans and shipping fees.

Mexico and Other Countries:

If you are ordering from outside the United States, please note that your check, money order, or international money transfer **must be payable in U.S. currency.** For speed, we ship international orders Air Parcel Post. Please refer to the chart for the correct shipping cost.

Domestic Shipping (stated in U.S. dollars)		
UPS Ground Service		$ 6.00
First Class Mail		8.00
Express Delivery Service Call For Details 1-800-235-5700		
International Shipping (stated in U.S. dollars)	One Set	Mult. Sets
Canada	$ 6.00	$ 9.75
Carribean Nations & Mexico	16.50	39.50
All Other Nations	18.50	50.00

ORDER TOLL FREE — 1-800-235-5700

Monday-Friday 8:00am to 5:00pm Eastern Time
Connecticut, Alaska, Hawaii, and all foreign residents
call 1-203-632-0500. Please have the
following at your fingertips before you call:

1. Your credit card number
2. The plan number
3. The order code number

Blueprint Order Form   Order Code # H91L3

GARLINGHOUSE

Plan No._____

❑ As Shown   ❑ Reversed

	Each	Amount
8 set pkg.	$215.00	$
5 set pkg.	$185.00	$
1 set pkg.	$140.00	$
____(Qty.) Add. sets @ $ 20.00		$
Material List	$ 20.00	$
Shipping — see chart		$
Subtotal		$
Sales Tax (CT residents add 8% sales tax, KS residents add 5.25% sales tax)		$
Total Amount Enclosed		$

Thank you for your order!

Garlinghouse plans are copyright protected. Purchaser hereby agrees that the home plan construction drawings being purchased will not be used for the construction of more than one single dwelling, and that these drawings will not be reproduced either in whole or in part by any means whatsoever.

Send your check, money order or credit card information to:

Garlinghouse Company
34 Industrial Park Place
Middletown, CT 06457

Bill To:

Name_____
(Please Print)
Address_____
City & State_____
Zip_____ Phone (   )_____

Ship To:

Name_____
Address_____
City & State_____
Zip_____ Phone (   )_____

Method of Payment: ❑ Check   ❑ Money Order

Charge To: ❑ Visa   ❑ Mastercard

Signature _____ Exp._____ / _____

Empty Nesters' Delight

No. 90546

Here's your opportunity to enjoy one-level living in an open plan. The covered entry leads three ways. The sunny kitchen to the left adjoins a cheerful breakfast nook, and features a built-in pantry. Straight ahead, the living and dining rooms, warmed by a fireplace flanked by windows and sliders to the back yard, flow together for a spacious feeling. The adjoining den can double as a third bedroom if you need it. To the right, a hallway leads to the bedroom wing containing convenient laundry facilities, two or three bedrooms, and two full baths. Notice the private dressing room and twin closets in the rear master suite.

**Living area — 1,377 sq. ft.
Garage — 2-car**

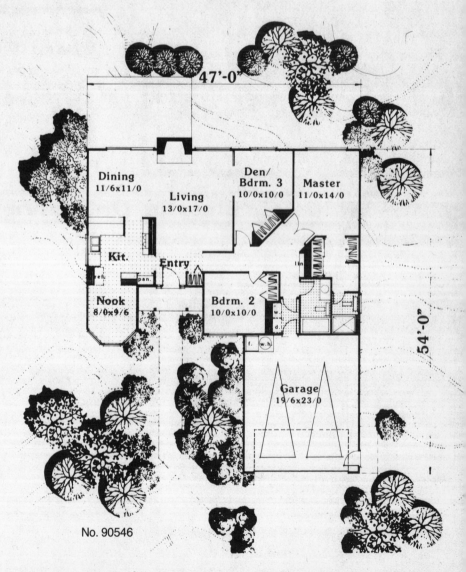

No. 90546